Math Practic
Grades 4-5

A Best Value Book™

Written by
Kelley Wingate Levy

Edited by
Aaron Levy

© Carson-Dellosa CD-3747

ISBN 0-88724-528-5

Table of Contents

Resource Pages

The drill pages in this book are designed to evaluate a student's ability based solely on current knowledge of the material. Most drill pages, therefore, do not include explanations or examples of exercises. The following resource pages contain supplementary information relevant to the types of problems students will encounter in this book. Representative problems are broken into steps and solved, and are accompanied by descriptions of the processes involved. Students, teachers, and parents are encouraged to refer to these resource pages for instruction and clarification of concepts presented in the drill pages.

Suggestions for resource page use:
- Reproduce the resource pages and distribute to students for guidance when solving problems.
- Enlarge example problems and display them while teaching. (Alternately, post them on a bulletin board, at a work station, or in another visible area.)
- Make a transparency of problems for display on an overhead projector. Use erasable markers to review the steps for solving problems.

Included in the back of this book are removable flash cards ideal for individual review, group solving sessions, or as part of timed, sequential, or grouping activities. Carefully pull out the flash cards and cut them apart using scissors or a paper cutter.

Resource Pages

Addition—without Regrouping

Solve.
142
+ 537

1. Add the ones column first.

1 4 2
+ 5 3 7
9

2. Add the tens column second.

1 4 2
+ 5 3 7
7 9

3. Add the hundreds column third.

1 4 2
+ 5 3 7
6 7 9

Addition—with Regrouping

Solve.
4,826
632
+ 5,567

1. Add the ones column first, then regroup.

4 8 2 6 → 6
6 3 2 → 2
+ 5 5 6 7 → 7
5 ①5

2. Add the tens column second, then regroup.

4 8 2 6 → 2
6 3 2 → 3
+ 5 5 6 7 → 6
1 5 ①1

3. Add the hundreds column third, then regroup.

4 8 2 6 → 8
6 3 2 → 6
+ 5 5 6 7 → 5
0 1 5 ②0

4. Continue to add and regroup.

2
4 8 2 6
6 3 2
+ 5 5 6 7
1 1 0 1 5

Subtraction—without Regrouping

Solve.
789
− 235

1. Subtract the ones column first.

7 8 9
− 2 3 5
4

2. Subtract the tens column second.

7 8 9
− 2 3 5
5 4

3. Subtract the hundreds column third.

7 8 9
− 2 3 5
5 5 4

Subtraction—with Regrouping

Solve.
91,542
− 8,367

1. To subtract the ones, borrow 1 ten from the 4 in the tens place. Rename the number 2 as 12 and subtract.

3 1
9 1 5 4 2
− 8 3 6 7
5

2. To subtract the tens, borrow 1 hundred from the 5 in the hundreds place. Rename the number 3 as 13 and subtract.

4 13 1
9 1 5 4 2
− 8 3 6 7
7 5

3. Continue to borrow, rename, and subtract.

8 1 4 13
9 1 5 4 2
− 8 3 6 7
8 3 1 7 5

Multiplication—without Regrouping

Solve.
134
x 2

1. Multiply 4 x 2.

1 3 ④
x ②
8

2. Multiply 3 x 2.

1 ③ 4
x ②
6 8

3. Multiply 1 x 2.

① 3 4
x ②
2 6 8

Multiplication—with Regrouping

Solve.
7,495
x   3

1. Multiply 5 x 3. Carry the 1 to the tens place.

$$5 \times 3$$

7 4 9 ⑤
x   ③
⑮
→ 5

2. Multiply 9 x 3, then add the 1 that was carried.

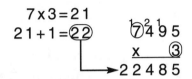

$9 \times 3 = 27$
$27 + 1 = ㉘$

7 4 ⑨ 5
x   ③
→ 8 5

3. Multiply 3 x 4, then add the 2 that was carried.

$3 \times 4 = 1 2$
$12 + 2 = ⑭$

7 ④ 9 5
x   ③
→ 4 8 5

4. Continue to multiply, carry, and add.

$7 \times 3 = 2 1$
$21 + 1 = ㉒$

⑦ 4 9 5
x   ③
→ 2 2 4 8 5

Division—with No Remainder

Solve.
5)620

1. ⑤ goes into six ① time.

```
    1
5)6 2 0
- 5
  1
```
Multiply 5 x 1 and subtract from 6.

2. Bring down the 2. 5 goes into twelve ② times.

```
   1 2
5)6 2 0
 - 5
   1 2
  - 1 0
     2
```

3. Bring down the 0. 5 goes into twenty ④ times.

```
   1 2 4
5)6 2 0
 - 5
   1 2
  - 1 0
     2 0
   - 2 0
       0
```

Division—with a Remainder

Solve.
6)437

1. Divide as usual.

```
   7 2 R5
6)4 3 7
 - 4 2
   1 7
  - 1 2
     5
```

Since 6 is too large to go into 5, this is the remainder.

Fractions—Changing Fractions to Simplest Form

Change $\frac{15}{20}$ to simplest form.

1. Divide 15 and 20 by their greatest common factor, 5.

$$\frac{15 \div 5}{20 \div 5} = \frac{3}{4}$$

$\frac{3}{4}$ is the simplest form for $\frac{15}{20}$ because 3 and 4 have no factors in common other than 1.

Fractions—Changing Fractions to Mixed Numbers

Change $\frac{10}{7}$ to simplest form.

A fraction can be changed to a mixed number when it names a number greater than 1. This is called an improper fraction.

1. Divide 10 by 7.

```
   1 R3
7)1 0
 - 7
   3
```

2. Since 7 goes into 10 once, the whole number will be 1. Since there is a remainder of 3, the remaining fraction is $\frac{3}{7}$. Therefore, the mixed number for $\frac{10}{7}$ is $1\frac{3}{7}$.

Fractions—Changing Mixed Numbers to Improper Fractions

Change $3\frac{1}{4}$ to simplest form.

1. Multiply the whole number, 3, by the denominator, 4.

$$3 \times 4 = 12$$

2. Add the numerator, 1, to 12.

$$12 + 1 = 13$$

3. 13 is now the new numerator. The denominator, 4, remains the same. Therefore, the improper fraction for $3\frac{1}{4}$ is $\frac{13}{4}$.

Fractions—Making Fractions Equivalent

Find a fraction equal to $\frac{1}{2}$.

To find an equivalent for a fraction, multiply the numerator and the denominator by the same number.

$$\frac{1 \times 4 = 4}{2 \times 4 = 8}$$

Therefore, $\frac{1}{2}$ is equal to $\frac{4}{8}$.

Fractions—Multiplying Fractions

Solve. $\frac{2}{3} \times \frac{3}{5}$

To multiply fractions, multiply the numerators and then multiply the denominators.

$$\frac{2}{3} \times \frac{3}{5} = \frac{2 \times 3 = 6}{3 \times 5 = 15}$$

Therefore, $\frac{2}{3} \times \frac{3}{5} = \frac{6}{15}$

Fractions—Multiplying Whole Numbers and Fractions

Solve. $3 \times \frac{1}{4}$

1. Rename the whole number as a fraction.

$$3 = \frac{3}{1}$$

2. Multiply the fractions.

$$\frac{3 \times 1 = 3}{1 \times 4 = 4}$$

Fractions—Multiplying Mixed Numbers and Whole Numbers

Solve. $3\frac{1}{5} \times 4$

1. Rename both the whole number and the mixed number as fractions.

$$3\frac{1}{5} = \frac{16}{5} \qquad 4 = \frac{4}{1}$$

2. Multiply the fractions.

$$\frac{16 \times 4}{5 \times 1} = \frac{64}{5}$$

3. Change to simplest form or a mixed number.

$$\frac{64}{5} = 12\frac{4}{5}$$

Fractions—Adding Fractions with the Same Denominators

Solve. $\frac{3}{8} + \frac{7}{8}$

1. Add the numerators, while keeping the denominators the same.

$$\frac{3 + 7}{8} = \frac{10}{8}$$

2. Change to simplest form or a mixed number when possible.

$$\frac{10}{8} = 1\frac{1}{4}$$

Fractions—Adding Fractions with Different Denominators

Solve. $\frac{3}{4} + \frac{2}{3}$

1. Rename the fractions so each has the same denominator.

$$\frac{3}{4} = \frac{9}{12} \quad \text{and} \quad \frac{2}{3} = \frac{8}{12}$$

2. Add the fractions that have been renamed.

$$\frac{9}{12} + \frac{8}{12} = \frac{17}{12}$$

3. Change to simplest form.

$$\frac{17}{12} = 1\frac{5}{12}$$

Fractions—Adding Mixed Numbers with Different Denominators

Solve. $4\frac{3}{5} + 2\frac{1}{2}$

1. Rename each mixed number so that the fractions have the same denominators.

$$4\frac{3}{5} = 4\frac{6}{10} \quad \text{and} \quad 2\frac{1}{2} = 2\frac{5}{10}$$

2. Rewrite the problem and solve.

$$4\frac{6}{10} + 2\frac{5}{10} = 6\frac{11}{10}$$

3. Change to simplest form.

$$6\frac{11}{10} = 7\frac{1}{10}$$

Fractions—Subtracting Fractions with the Same Denominators

Solve.
$\frac{5}{6} - \frac{1}{6}$

1. Subtract the numerators and keep the denominators the same.

$$\frac{5-1}{6} = \frac{4}{6}$$

2. Change to simplest form when possible.

$$\frac{4}{6} = \frac{2}{3}$$

Fractions—Subtracting Fractions from Whole Numbers

Solve.
$8 - \frac{4}{5}$

1. Rename the whole number so it is a fraction.

$$8 = \frac{8}{1}$$

2. Rename the fractions so they have the same denominator.

$$\frac{8}{1} - \frac{4}{5} = \frac{40}{5} - \frac{4}{5}$$

3. Subtract the fractions and change to simplest form or a mixed number.

$$\frac{40}{5} - \frac{4}{5} = \frac{36}{5} = 7\frac{1}{5}$$

Fractions—Subtracting Mixed Numbers with the Same Denominators

Solve.
$7\frac{2}{9} - 3\frac{7}{9}$

1. Rename $7\frac{2}{9}$ in order to subtract $3\frac{7}{9}$.

$$7\frac{2}{9} = 6 + 1\frac{2}{9} = 6\frac{11}{9}$$

2. Use the renamed fraction to rewrite the problem.

$$6\frac{11}{9} - 3\frac{7}{9} =$$

3. Subtract the whole numbers, then subtract the fractions.

$$6\frac{11}{9} - 3\frac{7}{9} = 3\frac{4}{9}$$

Fractions—Subtracting Fractions with Different Denominators

Solve.
$\frac{4}{5} - \frac{2}{3}$

1. Rename the fractions so they both have the same denominator.

$$\frac{4}{5} - \frac{2}{3} = \frac{12}{15} - \frac{10}{15}$$

2. Subtract the renamed fractions.

$$\frac{12}{15} - \frac{10}{15} = \frac{2}{15}$$

Fractions—Subtracting Mixed Numbers with Different Denominators

Solve.
$4\frac{1}{2} - 2\frac{3}{7}$

1. Rename the fractions so they both have the same denominator.

$$4\frac{1}{2} = 4\frac{7}{14} \qquad 2\frac{3}{7} = 2\frac{6}{14}$$

2. Rewrite the problem with the renamed mixed numbers and subtract.

$$4\frac{7}{14} - 2\frac{6}{14} = 2\frac{1}{14}$$

Decimals—Adding Decimals

Solve.
54.03 + 3.2 =

1. Line up the decimals first and add as usual.

```
 54.03
+3.2
 57.23
```

Decimals—Subtracting Decimals

Solve.
429.86 − 28.7=

1. Line up the decimals first and subtract as usual.

```
 429.86
− 28.7
 401.16
```

Decimals—Dividing Decimals

Solve.
$.06\overline{\smash{)}5.412}$

1. Count the number of digits to the right of the decimal point in the divisor (.06).

   .06 → 2 digits are to the right of the decimal

2. Move the decimal point in the dividend (5.412) to the right as many spaces as you counted in the divisor.

   $\overline{\smash{)}5\underset{\circ}{} 4 1.2}$

3. Divide as usual.

$$
\begin{array}{r}
9\ 0\ \ 2 \\
6\overline{\smash{)}5\ 4\ 1\ .\ 2} \\
-\underline{5\ 4} \\
0\ 1\ 2 \\
-\underline{1\ 2} \\
0
\end{array}
$$

4. Bring up the decimal point.

$$
\begin{array}{r}
9\ 0\ .\ 2 \\
6\overline{\smash{)}5\ 4\ 1\ .\ 2} \\
-\underline{5\ 4} \\
0\ 1\ 2 \\
-\underline{1\ 2} \\
0
\end{array}
$$

Changing Decimals to Fractions

To change a decimal to a fraction, use the decimal as a numerator over either the number 10, 100, 1,000, etc., depending on the number of digits after the decimal point. Change to simplest form. Study the chart below.

Examples:

Number of digits after decimal point	1	2	3
Denominator	10	100	1,000

$$0.5 = \frac{5}{10} = \frac{1}{2} \qquad 0.75 = \frac{75}{100} = \frac{3}{4} \qquad 0.125 = \frac{125}{1,000} = \frac{1}{8}$$

Changing Fractions to Decimals

To change a fraction to a decimal, divide the denominator into the numerator in the following manner.

1. If the numerator has one digit, place a decimal point just after the numerator as a dividend.

   Example: $\frac{4}{5} = 5\overline{\smash{)}4.0} = .8$

2. If the numerator has two digits, place a decimal point just after the second number of the numerator as a dividend.

   Example: $\frac{25}{125} = 125\overline{\smash{)}25.00} = .20$

Geometry—Lines and Line Segments

A **line** has no end points and is denoted in the following way:

To name a line, name any two points on the line. Line $\overleftrightarrow{AB}$ or Line $\overleftrightarrow{BA}$

A **line segment** has two end points and is denoted in the following way:

To name a line segment, name the end points. Line Segment $\overline{CD}$ or Line Segment $\overline{DC}$

Geometry—Angles and Polygons

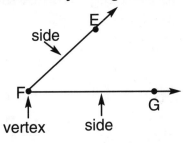

side E side F vertex G

Angle EFG, denoted by ∠EFG, has two sides and a vertex. To name an angle, use the vertex as the middle letter.

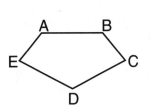

To name a polygon, use the letters of the vertices. Polygon ABCDE

Geometry—Circles

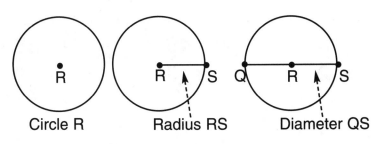

Circle R   Radius RS   Diameter QS

1. To name a **circle**, use the letter at the center point of the circle.
2. A **radius** is a line segment that goes from the center of a circle to a point on the circle.
3. A **diameter** is a line segment that has both of its end points on the circle and passes through the center point.

Geometry—Defining Polygons

Shape	No. of Sides
triangle	3
quadrilateral	4
pentagon	5
hexagon	6
heptagon	7
octagon	8

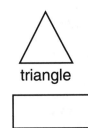

triangle

quadrilateral

pentagon

hexagon

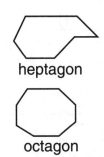

heptagon

octagon

Measurements—Units of Measure

Abbreviations		Equivalents
millimeter	mm	10 mm = 1 cm
centimeter	cm	100 cm = 1 m
meter	m	1,000 m = 1 km
kilometer	km	

Abbreviations		Equivalents
inch	in	12 in = 1 ft
foot	ft	3 ft = 1 yd
yard	yd	5,280 ft = 1 mi
mile	mi	1,760 yd = 1 mi

Measurements—Finding Perimeter and Area

To find the **perimeter** of a rectangle or square, add the length of each side.

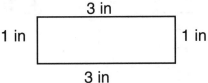

3 in
1 in   1 in
3 in

3 + 1 + 3 + 1 = 8 in

To find the **area** of a square or rectangle, multiply the length times the width.

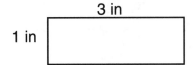

3 in
1 in

3 x 1 = 3 square in or 3 in²

Name_____   Skill: Adding One and Two Digit Numbers

Add.

1. 53
   + 6

2. 42
   + 7

3. 25
   + 3

4. 36
   + 2

5. 41
   + 7

6. 25
   + 5

7. 17
   + 9

8. 10
   + 2

9. 49
   + 8

10. 65
   + 9

11. 72
   + 6

12. 85
   + 4

13. 97
   + 2

14. 65
   + 1

15. 39
   + 4

16. 22
   + 6

17. 45
   + 3

18. 69
   + 8

19. 72
   + 4

20. 87
   + 9

21. 56
   + 4

22. 65
   + 8

23. 17
   + 7

24. 26
   + 7

25. 30
   + 8

26. 14
   + 9

27. 38
   + 6

28. 51
   + 7

29. 62
   + 4

30. 43
   + 5

Total Problems 30   Problems Correct ____

1

Name_____   Skill: Adding Two Digit Numbers

Add.

1. 36
   + 54

2. 42
   + 17

3. 85
   + 12

4. 99
   + 1

5. 25
   + 15

6. 53
   + 53

7. 22
   + 16

8. 36
   + 33

9. 79
   + 16

10. 42
    + 18

11. 12
    + 24

12. 60
    + 32

13. 48
    + 72

14. 63
    + 49

15. 89
    + 11

16. 51
    +19

17. 40
    + 30

18. 92
    + 86

19. 83
    + 25

20. 47
    + 39

21. 28
    + 27

22. 53
    + 10

23. 43
    + 21

24. 78
    + 65

25. 90
    + 62

26. 91
    + 33

27. 25
    + 25

28. 57
    + 31

29. 87
    + 14

30. 92
    + 27

Total Problems __30__ Problems Correct ____

2

Name_____   Skill: Adding Three and Four Digit Numbers

Add.

| 1. | 4,237
+ 201 | 2. | 5,968
+ 525 | 3. | 6,010
+ 902 | 4. | 7,546
+ 323 | 5. | 4,870
+ 106 |

| 6. | 9,841
+ 520 | 7. | 8,211
+ 345 | 8. | 9,076
+ 153 | 9. | 1,120
+ 782 | 10. | 2,436
+ 618 |

| 11. | 3,011
+ 654 | 12. | 8,432
+ 137 | 13. | 6,509
+ 225 | 14. | 6,029
+ 367 | 15. | 5,843
+ 492 |

| 16. | 4,472
+ 689 | 17. | 5,072
+ 549 | 18. | 2,389
+ 422 | 19. | 1,760
+ 195 | 20. | 7,352
+ 254 |

| 21. | 4,870
+ 287 | 22. | 6,580
+ 871 | 23. | 3,653
+ 321 | 24. | 4,661
+ 128 | 25. | 2,704
+ 202 |

Total Problems 25 Problems Correct ____

Name_____ Skill: Adding Three and Four Digit Numbers

Add.

1. 7,456   2. 5,057   3. 4,555   4. 9,879   5. 2,124
    + 214   + 421   + 701   + 256   + 578

6. 4,888   7. 6,244   8. 8,247   9. 3,121   10. 2,259
    + 247   + 652   + 920   + 322   + 621

11. 5,016   12. 8,885   13. 1,657   14. 2,456   15. 5,241
    + 214   + 546   + 111   + 108   + 568

16. 4,111   17. 2,255   18. 3,147   19. 1,852   20. 7,745
    + 287   + 303   + 434   + 369   + 325

21. 4,495   22. 7,843   23. 2,829   24. 3,715   25. 2,951
    + 712   + 367   + 197   + 246   + 314

Total Problems 25 Problems Correct ____

Name_____ Skill: Adding Three and Four Digit Numbers

Add.

1. 1,526
   + 718

2. 4,159
   + 936

3. 4,963
   + 173

4. 6,879
   + 316

5. 1,258
   + 648

6. 3,804
   + 207

7. 6,943
   + 309

8. 2,488
   + 395

9. 3,977
   + 478

10. 2,655
    + 165

11. 4,358
    + 885

12. 6,200
    + 356

13. 4,650
    + 121

14. 2,456
    + 522

15. 5,651
    + 786

16. 5,145
    + 788

17. 2,960
    + 785

18. 4,540
    + 124

19. 1,865
    + 750

20. 6,441
    + 220

21. 7,321
    + 992

22. 2,635
    + 223

23. 2,564
    + 852

24. 3,245
    + 321

25. 3,251
    + 775

Total Problems _25_ **Problems Correct** ____

Add.

1.	453	2.	987	3.	202	4.	376	5.	500
	125		642		169		825		627
	+ 678		+ 325		+ 584		+ 916		+ 220

6.	143	7.	942	8.	609	9.	210	10.	904
	225		787		333		422		409
	+ 336		+ 527		+ 175		+ 871		+ 105

11.	612	12.	240	13.	892	14.	275	15.	318
	717		135		357		245		771
	+ 246		+ 167		+ 418		+ 106		+ 522

16.	818	17.	954	18.	987	19.	123	20.	901
	529		623		789		497		801
	332		873		102		675		710
	+ 106		+ 480		+ 201		+ 542		+ 410

21.	533	22.	405	23.	220	24.	771	25.	147
	397		612		115		860		257
	864		935		780		550		662
	+ 702		+ 360		+ 650		+ 137		+ 770

Total Problems __25__ Problems Correct ____

Name_____

Add.

1. 2,671
       52
      125
   + 406

2.   35
       403
     3,850
   +   16

3.   17
        62
        54
   + 2,560

4. 8,430
      217
       32
   + 2,560

5.   97
       621
       503
   +   7

6. 7,732
      806
       54
   + 325

7. 6,210
    5,332
       15
   + 407

8. 3,275
    3,902
    7,340
   + 803

9. 3,243
    8,395
       43
   + 731

10. 6,035
       63
      532
   + 172

11. 5,306
       92
       24
   + 525

12. 2,591
    2,624
       33
   + 106

13. 4,305
      307
       34
   +   67

14. 9,876
    1,445
      324
   + 225

15. 3,298
      867
       54
   + 144

16. 8,214
      248
       17
   + 200

17. 9,200
        3
      146
   + 408

18. 3,084
       26
      192
   + 764

19.   21
       403
       809
   + 4,321

20.   726
        50
         4
   + 9,210

Total Problems 20 Problems Correct ____

7

Subtract.

1. $\begin{array}{r} 35 \\ -\ 5 \\ \hline \end{array}$
2. $\begin{array}{r} 42 \\ -\ 7 \\ \hline \end{array}$
3. $\begin{array}{r} 18 \\ -\ 9 \\ \hline \end{array}$
4. $\begin{array}{r} 27 \\ -\ 3 \\ \hline \end{array}$
5. $\begin{array}{r} 59 \\ -\ 8 \\ \hline \end{array}$

6. $\begin{array}{r} 62 \\ -\ 9 \\ \hline \end{array}$
7. $\begin{array}{r} 47 \\ -\ 8 \\ \hline \end{array}$
8. $\begin{array}{r} 25 \\ -\ 3 \\ \hline \end{array}$
9. $\begin{array}{r} 33 \\ -\ 5 \\ \hline \end{array}$
10. $\begin{array}{r} 49 \\ -\ 6 \\ \hline \end{array}$

11. $\begin{array}{r} 51 \\ -\ 7 \\ \hline \end{array}$
12. $\begin{array}{r} 62 \\ -\ 5 \\ \hline \end{array}$
13. $\begin{array}{r} 84 \\ -\ 5 \\ \hline \end{array}$
14. $\begin{array}{r} 92 \\ -\ 9 \\ \hline \end{array}$
15. $\begin{array}{r} 76 \\ -\ 7 \\ \hline \end{array}$

16. $\begin{array}{r} 64 \\ -\ 3 \\ \hline \end{array}$
17. $\begin{array}{r} 87 \\ -\ 5 \\ \hline \end{array}$
18. $\begin{array}{r} 97 \\ -\ 4 \\ \hline \end{array}$
19. $\begin{array}{r} 92 \\ -10 \\ \hline \end{array}$
20. $\begin{array}{r} 32 \\ -\ 6 \\ \hline \end{array}$

21. $\begin{array}{r} 25 \\ -14 \\ \hline \end{array}$
22. $\begin{array}{r} 88 \\ -27 \\ \hline \end{array}$
23. $\begin{array}{r} 95 \\ -64 \\ \hline \end{array}$
24. $\begin{array}{r} 75 \\ -43 \\ \hline \end{array}$
25. $\begin{array}{r} 53 \\ -2 \\ \hline \end{array}$

26. $\begin{array}{r} 73 \\ -62 \\ \hline \end{array}$
27. $\begin{array}{r} 86 \\ -29 \\ \hline \end{array}$
28. $\begin{array}{r} 32 \\ -28 \\ \hline \end{array}$
29. $\begin{array}{r} 56 \\ -26 \\ \hline \end{array}$
30. $\begin{array}{r} 28 \\ -3 \\ \hline \end{array}$

Total Problems __30__ Problems Correct ____

Name_____

Subtract.

1.
$$302 - 25$$

2.
$$604 - 52$$

3.
$$479 - 63$$

4.
$$527 - 49$$

5.
$$275 - 25$$

6.
$$800 - 72$$

7.
$$133 - 54$$

8.
$$175 - 87$$

9.
$$992 - 36$$

10.
$$689 - 56$$

11.
$$154 - 109$$

12.
$$387 - 275$$

13.
$$488 - 243$$

14.
$$767 - 516$$

15.
$$879 - 437$$

16.
$$2,487 - 333$$

17.
$$5,879 - 631$$

18.
$$1,250 - 758$$

19.
$$6,840 - 522$$

20.
$$3,807 - 416$$

21.
$$4,176 - 328$$

22.
$$5,912 - 756$$

23.
$$7,895 - 167$$

24.
$$1,786 - 250$$

25.
$$4,834 - 956$$

Total Problems __25__ Problems Correct ____

Name_____ Skill: Subtracting Four and Five
Digit Numbers

Subtract.

1. 30,821
    − 4,163

2. 52,964
    − 3,175

3. 87,576
    − 6,353

4. 83,542
    − 6,427

5. 72,541
    − 8,530

6. 76,283
    − 7,657

7. 94,443
    − 7,785

8. 62,083
    − 7,228

9. 44,785
    − 27,556

10. 35,463
    − 27,540

11. 46,724
    − 20,407

12. 72,450
    − 36,000

13. 42,165
    − 30,708

14. 40,081
    − 21,721

15. 31,621
    − 23,126

16. 92,140
    − 12,306

Total Problems 16 Problems Correct ____

10

Name_____

Multiply.

1. 2
   x 8

2. 4
   x 6

3. 10
   x 9

4. 6
   x 7

5. 11
   x 5

6. 8
   x 8

7. 3
   x 7

8. 4
   x 8

9. 9
   x 5

10. 3
    x 9

11. 10
    x 10

12. 11
    x 11

13. 4
    x 9

14. 3
    x 12

15. 11
    x 8

16. 7
    x 7

17. 6
    x 6

18. 5
    x 5

19. 3
    x 4

20. 10
    x 2

21. 3
    x 5

22. 2
    x 12

23. 1
    x 11

24. 4
    x 7

25. 5
    x 2

26. 12
    x 4

27. 6
    x 9

28. 15
    x 2

29. 13
    x 3

30. 18
    x 1

Total Problems 30   Problems Correct ____

Name_____

Multiply.

1. 12
x 12

2. 4
x 12

3. 3
x 6

4. 9
x 6

5. 11
x 7

6. 9
x 9

7. 4
x 10

8. 9
x 11

9. 7
x 12

10. 11
x 12

11. 2
x 9

12. 3
x 10

13. 8
x 9

14. 6
x 10

15. 10
x 11

16. 4
x 7

17. 5
x 12

18. 2
x 11

19. 6
x 12

20. 6
x 8

21. 3
x 11

22. 4
x 5

23. 12
x 11

24. 12
x 10

25. 5
x 10

26. 3
x 8

27. 4
x 4

28. 6
x 9

29. 9
x 9

30. 12
x 3

Total Problems _30_ Problems Correct ____

Multiply.

1. $\begin{array}{r} 10 \\ \times 11 \\ \hline \end{array}$
2. $\begin{array}{r} 5 \\ \times 13 \\ \hline \end{array}$
3. $\begin{array}{r} 4 \\ \times 5 \\ \hline \end{array}$
4. $\begin{array}{r} 8 \\ \times 2 \\ \hline \end{array}$
5. $\begin{array}{r} 10 \\ \times 5 \\ \hline \end{array}$

6. $\begin{array}{r} 7 \\ \times 10 \\ \hline \end{array}$
7. $\begin{array}{r} 5 \\ \times 11 \\ \hline \end{array}$
8. $\begin{array}{r} 6 \\ \times 10 \\ \hline \end{array}$
9. $\begin{array}{r} 4 \\ \times 10 \\ \hline \end{array}$
10. $\begin{array}{r} 17 \\ \times 12 \\ \hline \end{array}$

11. $\begin{array}{r} 1 \\ \times 9 \\ \hline \end{array}$
12. $\begin{array}{r} 3 \\ \times 8 \\ \hline \end{array}$
13. $\begin{array}{r} 5 \\ \times 9 \\ \hline \end{array}$
14. $\begin{array}{r} 7 \\ \times 10 \\ \hline \end{array}$
15. $\begin{array}{r} 8 \\ \times 11 \\ \hline \end{array}$

16. $\begin{array}{r} 3 \\ \times 7 \\ \hline \end{array}$
17. $\begin{array}{r} 4 \\ \times 11 \\ \hline \end{array}$
18. $\begin{array}{r} 3 \\ \times 10 \\ \hline \end{array}$
19. $\begin{array}{r} 1 \\ \times 12 \\ \hline \end{array}$
20. $\begin{array}{r} 2 \\ \times 8 \\ \hline \end{array}$

21. $\begin{array}{r} 4 \\ \times 15 \\ \hline \end{array}$
22. $\begin{array}{r} 3 \\ \times 14 \\ \hline \end{array}$
23. $\begin{array}{r} 8 \\ \times 11 \\ \hline \end{array}$
24. $\begin{array}{r} 6 \\ \times 10 \\ \hline \end{array}$
25. $\begin{array}{r} 5 \\ \times 12 \\ \hline \end{array}$

26. $\begin{array}{r} 1 \\ \times 8 \\ \hline \end{array}$
27. $\begin{array}{r} 2 \\ \times 4 \\ \hline \end{array}$
28. $\begin{array}{r} 3 \\ \times 9 \\ \hline \end{array}$
29. $\begin{array}{r} 9 \\ \times 8 \\ \hline \end{array}$
30. $\begin{array}{r} 1 \\ \times 4 \\ \hline \end{array}$

Total Problems 30 Problems Correct ____

13

Multiply.

1. 50
   x 5

2. 71
   x 4

3. 52
   x 3

4. 86
   x 1

5. 40
   x 6

6. 21
   x 3

7. 82
   x 4

8. 33
   x 3

9. 12
   x 4

10. 22
    x 3

11. 21
    x 4

12. 12
    x 3

13. 24
    x 2

14. 41
    x 8

15. 81
    x 7

16. 51
    x 4

17. 11
    x 3

18. 71
    x 6

19. 91
    x 5

20. 92
    x 0

21. 62
    x 3

22. 23
    x 3

23. 44
    x 2

24. 82
    x 3

25. 34
    x 2

26. 24
    x 2

27. 22
    x 4

28. 14
    x 2

29. 52
    x 4

30. 63
    x 3

Total Problems 30   Problems Correct ____

Name_____

Multiply.

1. 48
    x 9

2. 27
    x 4

3. 85
    x 3

4. 72
    x 8

5. 35
    x 6

6. 28
    x 3

7. 56
    x 2

8. 82
    x 7

9. 69
    x 3

10. 34
    x 3

11. 54
    x 8

12. 37
    x 5

13. 16
    x 4

14. 26
    x 5

15. 39
    x 7

16. 82
    x 6

17. 77
    x 7

18. 53
    x 8

19. 62
    x 5

20. 43
    x 6

21. 12
    x 7

22. 57
    x 4

23. 14
    x 9

24. 43
    x 4

25. 25
    x 2

26. 53
    x 5

27. 34
    x 9

28. 46
    x 5

29. 78
    x 6

30. 25
    x 7

Total Problems _30_ Problems Correct ____

15

Multiply.

1. 323
    x 5

2. 109
    x 4

3. 206
    x 5

4. 423
    x 6

5. 816
    x 2

6. 515
    x 4

7. 812
    x 8

8. 617
    x 7

9. 415
    x 2

10. 815
    x 7

11. 255
    x 4

12. 503
    x 3

13. 134
    x 6

14. 584
    x 3

15. 804
    x 6

16. 915
    x 2

17. 827
    x 3

18. 905
    x 5

19. 234
    x 5

20. 316
    x 7

21. 860
    x 2

22. 122
    x 8

23. 706
    x 4

24. 342
    x 5

25. 715
    x 4

26. 861
    x 9

27. 523
    x 6

28. 422
    x 5

29. 256
    x 5

30. 121
    x 9

Total Problems 30   Problems Correct ____

Name_____

Multiply.

1. 2,582 x 7	2. 4,108 x 2	3. 5,306 x 3	4. 1,029 x 5	5. 5,678 x 2
6. 3,232 x 4	7. 7,109 x 8	8. 6,241 x 7	9. 5,414 x 2	10. 4,610 x 5
11. 1,067 x 3	12. 2,000 x 6	13. 6,384 x 9	14. 6,501 x 7	15. 5,129 x 5
16. 3,610 x 4	17. 2,168 x 6	18. 4,634 x 2	19. 2,897 x 4	20. 3,162 x 4
21. 7,564 x 5	22. 6,528 x 9	23. 8,436 x 5	24. 7,152 x 4	25. 7,109 x 6
26. 5,831 x 4	27. 5,672 x 3	28. 5,691 x 5	29. 4,646 x 9	30. 4,862 x 7

Total Problems 30 Problems Correct ____

Name_____ Skill: Multiplying Two Digit Numbers

Multiply.

1. 41 x 18	2. 38 x 22	3. 64 x 47	4. 68 x 32	5. 72 x 43
6. 53 x 38	7. 36 x 12	8. 82 x 51	9. 42 x 18	10. 72 x 63
11. 53 x 46	12. 62 x 43	13. 25 x 17	14. 86 x 42	15. 83 x 27
16. 52 x 30	17. 81 x 72	18. 91 x 43	19. 35 x 28	20. 70 x 60
21. 86 x 75	22. 56 x 13	23. 49 x 28	24. 73 x 56	25. 54 x 27

Total Problems 25   Problems Correct ____

Name_____

Multiply.

1. 518
   x 42

2. 729
   x 56

3. 455
   x 31

4. 512
   x 60

5. 485
   x 21

6. 216
   x 10

7. 591
   x 19

8. 327
   x 35

9. 244
   x 32

10. 123
    x 46

11. 443
    x 33

12. 248
    x 75

13. 697
    x 46

14. 843
    x 12

15. 695
    x 61

16. 687
    x 51

17. 792
    x 43

18. 826
    x 26

19. 746
    x 37

20. 792
    x 49

21. 554
    x 53

22. 456
    x 14

23. 647
    x 18

24. 535
    x 79

25. 691
    x 24

Total Problems 25 Problems Correct ____

Name_____   Skill: Multiplying Three Digit Numbers

Multiply.

1. 654 x 132	2. 221 x 103	3. 416 x 122	4. 412 x 203	5. 321 x 324
6. 542 x 172	7. 365 x 184	8. 593 x 347	9. 827 x 579	10. 427 x 273
11. 323 x 247	12. 756 x 633	13. 724 x 377	14. 520 x 397	15. 678 x 459
16. 826 x 825	17. 236 x 420	18. 351 x 240	19. 630 x 141	20. 517 x 510
21. 340 x 285	22. 630 x 246	23. 577 x 290	24. 770 x 143	25. 370 x 237

Total Problems _25_ Problems Correct ____

Name_____ Skill: Dividing by One Digit Numbers
—No Remainders

Divide.

1. 3)12   2. 4)24   3. 5)10   4. 3)9   5. 2)8

6. 4)12   7. 5)15   8. 6)42   9. 6)54   10. 7)63

11. 8)48   12. 9)72   13. 7)42   14. 4)28   15. 8)56

16. 30 ÷ 5 = ____   17. 12 ÷ 6 = ____   18. 36 ÷ 9 = ____

19. 35 ÷ 7 = ____   20. 21 ÷ 7 = ____   21. 32 ÷ 4 = ____

22. 14 ÷ 7 = ____   23. 24 ÷ 6 = ____   24. 20 ÷ 5 = ____

25. 36 ÷ 9 = ____   26. 64 ÷ 8 = ____   27. 18 ÷ 6 = ____

Total Problems _27_ Problems Correct ____

Name_____ Skill: Dividing by One Digit Numbers
—No Remainders

Divide.

1. $6\overline{)72}$ 2. $7\overline{)98}$ 3. $3\overline{)36}$ 4. $2\overline{)24}$ 5. $8\overline{)80}$

6. $5\overline{)90}$ 7. $4\overline{)72}$ 8. $7\overline{)70}$ 9. $6\overline{)84}$ 10. $2\overline{)86}$

11. $3\overline{)93}$ 12. $7\overline{)91}$ 13. $8\overline{)88}$ 14. $9\overline{)99}$ 15. $4\overline{)96}$

16. $2\overline{)36}$ 17. $4\overline{)40}$ 18. $5\overline{)55}$ 19. $9\overline{)90}$ 20. $3\overline{)45}$

21. $3\overline{)96}$ 22. $7\overline{)84}$ 23. $5\overline{)55}$ 24. $3\overline{)75}$ 25. $5\overline{)85}$

26. $3\overline{)66}$ 27. $6\overline{)78}$ 28. $5\overline{)90}$ 29. $3\overline{)51}$ 30. $8\overline{)96}$

Total Problems _30_ Problems Correct ____

22

Name_____

Divide.

1. 9⟌1,368   2. 7⟌2,926   3. 6⟌2,706   4. 5⟌1,125

5. 4⟌1,228   6. 4⟌1,008   7. 3⟌2,019   8. 2⟌1,024

9. 8⟌5,392   10. 5⟌975   11. 3⟌1,008   12. 9⟌1,134

13. 6⟌1,878   14. 4⟌2,128   15. 8⟌3,888   16. 8⟌4,960

17. 5⟌1,395   18. 2⟌1,224   19. 7⟌1,421   20. 9⟌2,790

Total Problems 20   Problems Correct ____

23

Name_____   Skill: Dividing by One Digit Numbers
                                              —with Remainders

Divide.

1. $7\overline{)82}$ 2. $8\overline{)95}$ 3. $4\overline{)63}$ 4. $5\overline{)81}$ 5. $6\overline{)74}$

6. $4\overline{)54}$ 7. $4\overline{)18}$ 8. $5\overline{)22}$ 9. $4\overline{)41}$ 10. $8\overline{)37}$

11. $3\overline{)26}$ 12. $7\overline{)57}$ 13. $5\overline{)18}$ 14. $3\overline{)29}$ 15. $5\overline{)42}$

16. $23 \div 5 =$ _____   17. $45 \div 6 =$ _____   18. $25 \div 3 =$ _____

19. $58 \div 7 =$ _____   20. $51 \div 7 =$ _____   21. $43 \div 2 =$ _____

22. $46 \div 5 =$ _____   23. $32 \div 6 =$ _____   24. $19 \div 2 =$ _____

25. $24 \div 7 =$ _____   26. $26 \div 3 =$ _____   27. $87 \div 9 =$ _____

Total Problems __27__ Problems Correct ____

24

Divide.

1. 6⟌82   2. 3⟌59   3. 4⟌97   4. 5⟌63   5. 3⟌67

6. 2⟌39   7. 6⟌82   8. 8⟌97   9. 5⟌83   10. 5⟌63

11. 8⟌89   12. 2⟌81   13. 7⟌92   14. 7⟌81   15. 6⟌73

16. 4⟌85   17. 2⟌23   18. 7⟌93   19. 6⟌85   20. 3⟌83

21. 4⟌70   22. 8⟌94   23. 7⟌79   24. 6⟌89   25. 7⟌85

26. 7⟌93   27. 5⟌82   28. 6⟌89   29. 9⟌98   30. 3⟌47

Total Problems _30_ Problems Correct ____

Name_____

Divide.

1. $4\overline{)873}$ 2. $5\overline{)527}$ 3. $3\overline{)784}$ 4. $4\overline{)862}$

5. $5\overline{)943}$ 6. $2\overline{)597}$ 7. $4\overline{)486}$ 8. $2\overline{)733}$

9. $8\overline{)957}$ 10. $9\overline{)973}$ 11. $3\overline{)629}$ 12. $8\overline{)937}$

13. $9\overline{)987}$ 14. $4\overline{)574}$ 15. $2\overline{)301}$ 16. $3\overline{)574}$

17. $7\overline{)915}$ 18. $6\overline{)653}$ 19. $5\overline{)637}$ 20. $4\overline{)653}$

Total Problems _20_ Problems Correct ____

Name_____

Divide.

1. 32 ⟌ 512   2. 41 ⟌ 820   3. 15 ⟌ 540   4. 26 ⟌ 338

5. 52 ⟌ 624   6. 12 ⟌ 144   7. 73 ⟌ 365   8. 25 ⟌ 350

9. 18 ⟌ 450   10. 32 ⟌ 960   11. 56 ⟌ 952   12. 45 ⟌ 990

13. 32 ⟌ 768   14. 18 ⟌ 702   15. 47 ⟌ 517   16. 24 ⟌ 600

17. 62 ⟌ 992   18. 39 ⟌ 858   19. 27 ⟌ 810   20. 54 ⟌ 864

Total Problems 20   Problems Correct ____

27

Name_____

Divide.

1. $67\overline{)807}$ 2. $58\overline{)368}$ 3. $25\overline{)465}$ 4. $45\overline{)787}$

5. $37\overline{)369}$ 6. $18\overline{)652}$ 7. $11\overline{)505}$ 8. $22\overline{)268}$

9. $64\overline{)654}$ 10. $23\overline{)875}$ 11. $19\overline{)410}$ 12. $42\overline{)632}$

13. $81\overline{)921}$ 14. $13\overline{)235}$ 15. $32\overline{)458}$ 16. $56\overline{)647}$

17. $61\overline{)741}$ 18. $40\overline{)142}$ 19. $53\overline{)367}$ 20. $87\overline{)357}$

Total Problems __20__ Problems Correct ____

Name_____

Divide.

1. 43$\overline{)1,256}$ 2. 21$\overline{)3,010}$ 3. 30$\overline{)6,172}$ 4. 59$\overline{)8,787}$

5. 48$\overline{)2,541}$ 6. 39$\overline{)8,563}$ 7. 78$\overline{)5,000}$ 8. 55$\overline{)9,999}$

9. 65$\overline{)1,596}$ 10. 82$\overline{)4,512}$ 11. 77$\overline{)2,159}$ 12. 27$\overline{)3,265}$

13. 22$\overline{)7,321}$ 14. 37$\overline{)2,148}$ 15. 85$\overline{)3,578}$ 16. 56$\overline{)5,892}$

Total Problems __16__ Problems Correct ____

Name_____ Skill: Learning about Fractions

Shade in the part of each shape that equals the given fraction.

1. $\dfrac{1}{2}$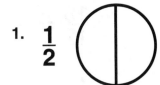

2. $\dfrac{3}{4}$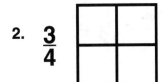

3. $\dfrac{2}{5}$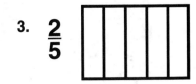

4. $\dfrac{2}{3}$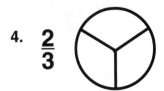

5. $\dfrac{7}{8}$

6. $\dfrac{5}{6}$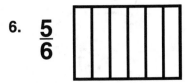

Write a fraction for each of the following.

7. Denominator 3, Numerator 2 _____

8. Numerator 7, Denominator 9 _____

9. Numerator 5, Denominator 6 _____

10. Denominator 8, Numerator 1 _____

11. Four-fifths _____

12. Three-fourths _____

Fill in the circle with >, <, or = to make each statement true.

13. $\dfrac{6}{5}$ ◯ 1 14. $\dfrac{7}{7}$ ◯ 1 15. $\dfrac{5}{8}$ ◯ 1 16. $\dfrac{3}{3}$ ◯ 1 17. $\dfrac{10}{6}$ ◯ 1

18. $\dfrac{1}{2}$ ◯ 1 19. $\dfrac{3}{7}$ ◯ 1 20. $\dfrac{8}{2}$ ◯ 1 21. $\dfrac{2}{2}$ ◯ 1 22. $\dfrac{7}{5}$ ◯ 1

Total Problems 22   Problems Correct ____

Name_____ Skill: Changing Fractions to Simplest Form

Change each fraction to simplest form.

1. $\dfrac{6}{8}$ =

2. $\dfrac{5}{20}$ =

3. $\dfrac{3}{12}$ =

4. $\dfrac{2}{8}$ =

5. $\dfrac{10}{12}$ =

6. $\dfrac{3}{24}$ =

7. $\dfrac{4}{8}$ =

8. $\dfrac{5}{15}$ =

9. $\dfrac{14}{21}$ =

10. $\dfrac{16}{24}$ =

11. $\dfrac{20}{35}$ =

12. $\dfrac{4}{16}$ =

13. $\dfrac{8}{16}$ =

14. $\dfrac{12}{16}$ =

15. $\dfrac{6}{18}$ =

16. $\dfrac{15}{20}$ =

17. $\dfrac{6}{9}$ =

18. $\dfrac{7}{21}$ =

19. $\dfrac{16}{32}$ =

20. $\dfrac{5}{10}$ =

21. $\dfrac{10}{20}$ =

22. $\dfrac{4}{16}$ =

23. $\dfrac{5}{25}$ =

24. $\dfrac{7}{35}$ =

25. $\dfrac{24}{32}$ =

26. $\dfrac{6}{16}$ =

27. $\dfrac{3}{15}$ =

28. $\dfrac{15}{30}$ =

29. $\dfrac{17}{34}$ =

30. $\dfrac{20}{40}$ =

Total Problems 30   Problems Correct ____

Skill: Changing Fractions to Simplest Form

Change each fraction to simplest form.

1. $\dfrac{4}{8} =$

2. $\dfrac{4}{12} =$

3. $\dfrac{3}{9} =$

4. $\dfrac{2}{4} =$

5. $\dfrac{12}{15} =$

6. $\dfrac{7}{14} =$

7. $\dfrac{2}{8} =$

8. $\dfrac{8}{24} =$

9. $\dfrac{15}{21} =$

10. $\dfrac{18}{24} =$

11. $\dfrac{20}{30} =$

12. $\dfrac{5}{30} =$

13. $\dfrac{8}{20} =$

14. $\dfrac{12}{30} =$

15. $\dfrac{4}{18} =$

16. $\dfrac{10}{28} =$

17. $\dfrac{3}{9} =$

18. $\dfrac{6}{18} =$

19. $\dfrac{20}{22} =$

20. $\dfrac{5}{15} =$

21. $\dfrac{14}{40} =$

22. $\dfrac{2}{6} =$

23. $\dfrac{5}{20} =$

24. $\dfrac{7}{28} =$

25. $\dfrac{15}{50} =$

26. $\dfrac{6}{20} =$

27. $\dfrac{3}{15} =$

28. $\dfrac{15}{20} =$

29. $\dfrac{16}{32} =$

30. $\dfrac{21}{45} =$

Total Problems 30   Problems Correct ____

Fill in the circle with >, <, or = to make each statement true.

1. $\dfrac{16}{52} \bigcirc \dfrac{16}{25}$

2. $\dfrac{4}{5} \bigcirc \dfrac{5}{6}$

3. $\dfrac{7}{8} \bigcirc \dfrac{5}{9}$

4. $\dfrac{13}{21} \bigcirc \dfrac{10}{13}$

5. $\dfrac{9}{10} \bigcirc \dfrac{8}{15}$

6. $\dfrac{1}{2} \bigcirc \dfrac{24}{50}$

7. $\dfrac{16}{20} \bigcirc \dfrac{10}{25}$

8. $\dfrac{12}{24} \bigcirc \dfrac{2}{4}$

9. $\dfrac{18}{21} \bigcirc \dfrac{12}{28}$

10. $\dfrac{12}{32} \bigcirc \dfrac{12}{24}$

11. $\dfrac{9}{15} \bigcirc \dfrac{4}{10}$

12. $\dfrac{9}{12} \bigcirc \dfrac{15}{20}$

13. $\dfrac{14}{16} \bigcirc \dfrac{15}{20}$

14. $\dfrac{6}{15} \bigcirc \dfrac{4}{20}$

15. $\dfrac{35}{39} \bigcirc \dfrac{14}{24}$

16. $\dfrac{56}{88} \bigcirc \dfrac{25}{55}$

17. $\dfrac{16}{36} \bigcirc \dfrac{24}{27}$

18. $\dfrac{16}{24} \bigcirc \dfrac{20}{30}$

19. $\dfrac{16}{16} \bigcirc \dfrac{25}{25}$

20. $\dfrac{25}{30} \bigcirc \dfrac{3}{18}$

21. $\dfrac{21}{35} \bigcirc \dfrac{16}{24}$

Total Problems _21_ Problems Correct ____

Name_____ Skill: Changing Fractions to Mixed Numbers

Change each improper fraction to a mixed number.

1. $\dfrac{4}{3}$ =

2. $\dfrac{5}{3}$ =

3. $\dfrac{10}{4}$ =

4. $\dfrac{6}{4}$ =

5. $\dfrac{10}{3}$ =

6. $\dfrac{20}{15}$ =

7. $\dfrac{12}{5}$ =

8. $\dfrac{19}{2}$ =

9. $\dfrac{43}{7}$ =

10. $\dfrac{24}{10}$ =

11. $\dfrac{7}{4}$ =

12. $\dfrac{13}{4}$ =

13. $\dfrac{27}{5}$ =

14. $\dfrac{19}{11}$ =

15. $\dfrac{9}{8}$ =

16. $\dfrac{55}{12}$ =

17. $\dfrac{13}{4}$ =

18. $\dfrac{15}{4}$ =

19. $\dfrac{20}{7}$ =

20. $\dfrac{16}{3}$ =

21. $\dfrac{18}{5}$ =

22. $\dfrac{13}{2}$ =

23. $\dfrac{8}{3}$ =

24. $\dfrac{9}{4}$ =

25. $\dfrac{10}{3}$ =

26. $\dfrac{5}{2}$ =

27. $\dfrac{17}{9}$ =

28. $\dfrac{15}{8}$ =

29. $\dfrac{17}{4}$ =

30. $\dfrac{50}{6}$ =

Total Problems _30_ Problems Correct ____

Change each improper fraction to a mixed number.

1. $\dfrac{6}{4} =$ 2. $\dfrac{7}{4} =$ 3. $\dfrac{11}{3} =$ 4. $\dfrac{8}{3} =$ 5. $\dfrac{12}{5} =$

6. $\dfrac{21}{12} =$ 7. $\dfrac{13}{3} =$ 8. $\dfrac{17}{4} =$ 9. $\dfrac{33}{6} =$ 10. $\dfrac{18}{11} =$

11. $\dfrac{9}{4} =$ 12. $\dfrac{14}{8} =$ 13. $\dfrac{19}{2} =$ 14. $\dfrac{14}{8} =$ 15. $\dfrac{9}{2} =$

16. $\dfrac{25}{11} =$ 17. $\dfrac{16}{5} =$ 18. $\dfrac{25}{3} =$ 19. $\dfrac{21}{8} =$ 20. $\dfrac{15}{4} =$

21. $\dfrac{19}{5} =$ 22. $\dfrac{13}{3} =$ 23. $\dfrac{8}{3} =$ 24. $\dfrac{7}{4} =$ 25. $\dfrac{10}{6} =$

26. $\dfrac{3}{2} =$ 27. $\dfrac{14}{8} =$ 28. $\dfrac{11}{6} =$ 29. $\dfrac{13}{3} =$ 30. $\dfrac{10}{4} =$

Total Problems __30__ Problems Correct ____

Name_____ Skill: Changing Fractions to Mixed Numbers

Change each improper fraction to a mixed number.

1. $\dfrac{9}{2}$ =

2. $\dfrac{12}{5}$ =

3. $\dfrac{11}{2}$ =

4. $\dfrac{16}{3}$ =

5. $\dfrac{11}{5}$ =

6. $\dfrac{51}{10}$ =

7. $\dfrac{13}{7}$ =

8. $\dfrac{17}{6}$ =

9. $\dfrac{12}{5}$ =

10. $\dfrac{15}{14}$ =

11. $\dfrac{19}{5}$ =

12. $\dfrac{16}{9}$ =

13. $\dfrac{25}{8}$ =

14. $\dfrac{3}{2}$ =

15. $\dfrac{6}{5}$ =

16. $\dfrac{8}{7}$ =

17. $\dfrac{10}{6}$ =

18. $\dfrac{11}{10}$ =

19. $\dfrac{61}{3}$ =

20. $\dfrac{15}{14}$ =

21. $\dfrac{14}{13}$ =

22. $\dfrac{17}{7}$ =

23. $\dfrac{19}{18}$ =

24. $\dfrac{13}{12}$ =

25. $\dfrac{19}{11}$ =

26. $\dfrac{8}{5}$ =

27. $\dfrac{13}{11}$ =

28. $\dfrac{26}{22}$ =

29. $\dfrac{47}{13}$ =

30. $\dfrac{10}{9}$ =

Total Problems 30 Problems Correct ____

Name_____ Skill: Changing Fractions to Mixed Numbers

Change each improper fraction to a mixed number or whole number.

1. $\dfrac{23}{15}$ =

2. $\dfrac{32}{15}$ =

3. $\dfrac{48}{5}$ =

4. $\dfrac{26}{4}$ =

5. $\dfrac{29}{7}$ =

6. $\dfrac{40}{24}$ =

7. $\dfrac{89}{17}$ =

8. $\dfrac{66}{50}$ =

9. $\dfrac{44}{13}$ =

10. $\dfrac{62}{9}$ =

11. $\dfrac{97}{33}$ =

12. $\dfrac{26}{15}$ =

13. $\dfrac{13}{3}$ =

14. $\dfrac{24}{20}$ =

15. $\dfrac{8}{3}$ =

16. $\dfrac{55}{12}$ =

17. $\dfrac{13}{4}$ =

18. $\dfrac{15}{3}$ =

19. $\dfrac{20}{7}$ =

20. $\dfrac{16}{3}$ =

21. $\dfrac{26}{12}$ =

22. $\dfrac{59}{25}$ =

23. $\dfrac{6}{4}$ =

24. $\dfrac{17}{6}$ =

25. $\dfrac{20}{8}$ =

26. $\dfrac{36}{34}$ =

27. $\dfrac{10}{8}$ =

28. $\dfrac{64}{49}$ =

29. $\dfrac{56}{11}$ =

30. $\dfrac{35}{12}$ =

Total Problems __30__ Problems Correct ____

37

Skill: Changing Mixed Numbers to
Improper Fractions

Change each mixed number to an improper fraction.

1. $3\frac{1}{2} =$

2. $4\frac{3}{8} =$

3. $6\frac{5}{7} =$

4. $5\frac{7}{8} =$

5. $8\frac{2}{3} =$

6. $10\frac{3}{5} =$

7. $7\frac{4}{5} =$

8. $2\frac{2}{3} =$

9. $4\frac{5}{9} =$

10. $1\frac{1}{10} =$

11. $2\frac{4}{9} =$

12. $12\frac{13}{15} =$

13. $6\frac{5}{8} =$

14. $4\frac{3}{4} =$

15. $3\frac{1}{3} =$

16. $5\frac{2}{3} =$

17. $2\frac{3}{8} =$

18. $4\frac{2}{3} =$

19. $9\frac{1}{2} =$

20. $4\frac{2}{4} =$

21. $6\frac{1}{5} =$

Total Problems 21 Problems Correct ____

38

Change each mixed number to an improper fraction.

1. $1\frac{2}{3} =$

2. $9\frac{6}{8} =$

3. $15\frac{3}{4} =$

4. $10\frac{5}{6} =$

5. $9\frac{2}{8} =$

6. $7\frac{10}{16} =$

7. $5\frac{4}{5} =$

8. $20\frac{2}{8} =$

9. $11\frac{3}{9} =$

10. $2\frac{1}{12} =$

11. $8\frac{3}{9} =$

12. $7\frac{5}{6} =$

13. $12\frac{4}{5} =$

14. $3\frac{3}{8} =$

15. $3\frac{2}{5} =$

16. $1\frac{1}{5} =$

17. $2\frac{3}{4} =$

18. $6\frac{1}{3} =$

19. $7\frac{1}{6} =$

20. $1\frac{1}{4} =$

21. $7\frac{2}{5} =$

Total Problems __21__ **Problems Correct** ____

Make each pair of fractions equivalent.

1. $\dfrac{2}{3} = \dfrac{}{12}$ 2. $\dfrac{3}{4} = \dfrac{}{16}$ 3. $\dfrac{2}{5} = \dfrac{}{10}$ 4. $\dfrac{1}{6} = \dfrac{}{12}$

5. $\dfrac{8}{9} = \dfrac{}{54}$ 6. $\dfrac{1}{2} = \dfrac{}{12}$ 7. $\dfrac{3}{8} = \dfrac{}{16}$ 8. $\dfrac{4}{5} = \dfrac{}{20}$

9. $\dfrac{1}{2} = \dfrac{}{10}$ 10. $\dfrac{4}{5} = \dfrac{}{25}$ 11. $\dfrac{5}{8} = \dfrac{}{24}$ 12. $\dfrac{3}{7} = \dfrac{}{21}$

13. $\dfrac{1}{8} = \dfrac{}{32}$ 14. $\dfrac{2}{5} = \dfrac{}{30}$ 15. $\dfrac{3}{4} = \dfrac{}{24}$ 16. $\dfrac{5}{6} = \dfrac{}{42}$

17. $\dfrac{4}{9} = \dfrac{}{81}$ 18. $\dfrac{7}{8} = \dfrac{}{64}$ 19. $\dfrac{3}{5} = \dfrac{}{15}$ 20. $\dfrac{1}{6} = \dfrac{}{36}$

21. $\dfrac{2}{9} = \dfrac{}{18}$ 22. $\dfrac{2}{3} = \dfrac{}{15}$ 23. $\dfrac{3}{7} = \dfrac{}{14}$ 24. $\dfrac{5}{8} = \dfrac{}{40}$

Total Problems 24   Problems Correct ____

Name_____ Skill: Making Fractions Equivalent

Complete each row by filling in the numerators, making each fraction equivalent to the first one.

1. $\frac{3}{4} = \frac{}{24} = \frac{}{16} = \frac{}{8} = \frac{}{20} = \frac{}{36}$

2. $\frac{1}{3} = \frac{}{9} = \frac{}{27} = \frac{}{90} = \frac{}{6} = \frac{}{12}$

3. $\frac{2}{5} = \frac{}{50} = \frac{}{10} = \frac{}{40} = \frac{}{15} = \frac{}{25}$

4. $\frac{1}{2} = \frac{}{36} = \frac{}{18} = \frac{}{16} = \frac{}{42} = \frac{}{48}$

5. $\frac{7}{8} = \frac{}{16} = \frac{}{56} = \frac{}{24} = \frac{}{48} = \frac{}{32}$

6. $\frac{3}{7} = \frac{}{21} = \frac{}{42} = \frac{}{14} = \frac{}{35} = \frac{}{28}$

7. $\frac{4}{9} = \frac{}{18} = \frac{}{45} = \frac{}{36} = \frac{}{54} = \frac{}{27}$

8. $\frac{5}{6} = \frac{}{48} = \frac{}{12} = \frac{}{30} = \frac{}{18} = \frac{}{24}$

Total Problems _8_ Problems Correct ____

41

Make each equivalent.

1. $4 = \dfrac{}{3}$

2. $\dfrac{1}{2} = \dfrac{}{8}$

3. $\dfrac{1}{3} = \dfrac{}{6}$

4. $\dfrac{2}{5} = \dfrac{}{10}$

5. $6 = \dfrac{}{5}$

6. $4 = \dfrac{}{2}$

7. $\dfrac{5}{6} = \dfrac{}{24}$

8. $\dfrac{7}{8} = \dfrac{}{64}$

9. $\dfrac{2}{3} = \dfrac{}{18}$

10. $3 = \dfrac{}{2}$

11. $2 = \dfrac{}{4}$

12. $\dfrac{2}{3} = \dfrac{}{15}$

13. $\dfrac{1}{5} = \dfrac{}{20}$

14. $\dfrac{5}{8} = \dfrac{}{40}$

15. $\dfrac{1}{4} = \dfrac{}{16}$

16. $\dfrac{3}{5} = \dfrac{}{15}$

17. $\dfrac{5}{6} = \dfrac{}{48}$

18. $\dfrac{1}{3} = \dfrac{}{36}$

19. $\dfrac{1}{8} = \dfrac{}{64}$

20. $\dfrac{3}{4} = \dfrac{}{24}$

21. $\dfrac{1}{6} = \dfrac{}{36}$

22. $\dfrac{2}{7} = \dfrac{}{49}$

23. $\dfrac{2}{5} = \dfrac{}{30}$

24. $\dfrac{7}{8} = \dfrac{}{56}$

Total Problems 24   Problems Correct _____

Name_____

Add the fractions and write the answers in simplest form.

1. $\dfrac{1}{3} + \dfrac{2}{3} =$

2. $\dfrac{1}{2} + \dfrac{1}{2} =$

3. $\dfrac{3}{5} + \dfrac{2}{5} =$

4. $\dfrac{2}{9} + \dfrac{5}{9} =$

5. $\dfrac{5}{8} + \dfrac{3}{8} =$

6. $\dfrac{3}{7} + \dfrac{2}{7} =$

7. $\dfrac{1}{6} + \dfrac{1}{6} =$

8. $\dfrac{5}{5} + \dfrac{2}{5} =$

9. $\dfrac{1}{3} + \dfrac{2}{3} =$

10. $\dfrac{3}{6} + \dfrac{1}{6} =$

11. $\dfrac{2}{10} + \dfrac{4}{10} =$

12. $\dfrac{1}{7} + \dfrac{1}{7} =$

13. $\dfrac{2}{4} + \dfrac{2}{4} =$

14. $\dfrac{1}{2} + \dfrac{1}{2} =$

15. $\dfrac{1}{6} + \dfrac{4}{6} =$

Total Problems __15__ Problems Correct _____

Name_____

Add the fractions and write the answers in simplest form.

1. $\dfrac{2}{7}$
    $+\ \dfrac{3}{7}$

2. $\dfrac{1}{5}$
    $+\ \dfrac{3}{5}$

3. $\dfrac{4}{8}$
    $+\ \dfrac{2}{8}$

4. $\dfrac{2}{10}$
    $+\ \dfrac{4}{10}$

5. $\dfrac{2}{6}$
    $+\ \dfrac{1}{6}$

6. $\dfrac{6}{8}$
    $+\ \dfrac{1}{8}$

7. $\dfrac{3}{5}$
    $+\ \dfrac{3}{5}$

8. $\dfrac{6}{7}$
    $+\ \dfrac{5}{7}$

9. $\dfrac{3}{4}$
    $+\ \dfrac{2}{4}$

10. $\dfrac{2}{9}$
    $+\ \dfrac{1}{9}$

11. $\dfrac{7}{10}$
    $+\ \dfrac{9}{10}$

12. $\dfrac{1}{4}$
    $+\ \dfrac{2}{4}$

13. $\dfrac{1}{8}$
    $+\ \dfrac{5}{8}$

14. $\dfrac{2}{3}$
    $+\ \dfrac{1}{3}$

15. $\dfrac{5}{12}$
    $+\ \dfrac{5}{12}$

16. $\dfrac{3}{7}$
    $+\ \dfrac{1}{7}$

17. $\dfrac{1}{5}$
    $+\ \dfrac{3}{5}$

18. $\dfrac{2}{8}$
    $+\ \dfrac{4}{8}$

19. $\dfrac{4}{9}$
    $+\ \dfrac{3}{9}$

20. $\dfrac{1}{6}$
    $+\ \dfrac{3}{6}$

Total Problems __20__ Problems Correct ____

Name_____

Add and write the answers in simplest form.

1. $1\frac{2}{5} + 2\frac{3}{5} =$

2. $6\frac{5}{8} + 7\frac{2}{8} =$

3. $2\frac{3}{4} + 2\frac{1}{4} =$

4. $5\frac{2}{7} + 6\frac{4}{7} =$

5. $3\frac{3}{8} + 4\frac{1}{8} =$

6. $5\frac{11}{15} + 6\frac{10}{15} =$

7. $3\frac{3}{8} + 4\frac{1}{8} =$

8. $8\frac{2}{5} + 1\frac{2}{5} =$

9. $2\frac{2}{5} + 2\frac{2}{5} =$

10. $4\frac{2}{9} + 5\frac{3}{9} =$

11. $7\frac{1}{8} + 7\frac{1}{8} =$

12. $4\frac{3}{4} + 1\frac{1}{4} =$

Total Problems __12__ Problems Correct ____

Name_____

Add and write the answers in simplest form.

1. $4\frac{5}{8}$
    $+\ 5\frac{4}{8}$
    _____

2. $1\frac{1}{2}$
    $+\ 4\frac{1}{2}$
    _____

3. $6\frac{2}{3}$
    $+\ 7\frac{2}{3}$
    _____

4. $3\frac{9}{10}$
    $+\ 7\frac{6}{10}$
    _____

5. $2\frac{2}{5}$
    $+\ 6\frac{4}{5}$
    _____

6. $8\frac{4}{9}$
    $+\ 1\frac{5}{9}$
    _____

7. $4\frac{2}{7}$
    $+\ 5\frac{3}{7}$
    _____

8. $3\frac{1}{3}$
    $+\ 4\frac{2}{3}$
    _____

9. $4\frac{5}{8}$
    $+\ 5\frac{4}{8}$
    _____

10. $8\frac{4}{9}$
    $+\ 1\frac{5}{9}$
    _____

11. $4\frac{2}{7}$
    $+\ 6\frac{3}{7}$
    _____

12. $3\frac{1}{3}$
    $+\ 4\frac{2}{3}$
    _____

13. $10\frac{3}{4}$
    $+\ 8\frac{2}{4}$
    _____

14. $2\frac{5}{6}$
    $+\ 8\frac{5}{6}$
    _____

15. $9\frac{4}{12}$
    $+\ 6\frac{10}{12}$
    _____

16. $1\frac{4}{5}$
    $+\ 5\frac{3}{5}$
    _____

Total Problems __16__ Problems Correct ____

Add and write the answers in simplest form.

1. $\dfrac{7}{8}$
    $+ \dfrac{1}{4}$

2. $\dfrac{3}{10}$
    $+ \dfrac{4}{5}$

3. $\dfrac{1}{4}$
    $+ \dfrac{1}{2}$

4. $\dfrac{1}{10}$
    $+ \dfrac{4}{8}$

5. $\dfrac{2}{3}$
    $+ \dfrac{5}{6}$

6. $\dfrac{1}{3}$
    $+ \dfrac{5}{6}$

7. $\dfrac{1}{12}$
    $+ \dfrac{3}{4}$

8. $\dfrac{2}{3}$
    $+ \dfrac{4}{9}$

9. $\dfrac{5}{8}$
    $+ \dfrac{1}{2}$

10. $\dfrac{5}{12}$
    $+ \dfrac{1}{4}$

11. $\dfrac{5}{12}$
    $+ \dfrac{1}{10}$

12. $\dfrac{2}{5}$
    $+ \dfrac{5}{10}$

13. $\dfrac{1}{8}$
    $+ \dfrac{5}{9}$

14. $\dfrac{2}{3}$
    $+ \dfrac{1}{6}$

15. $\dfrac{6}{12}$
    $+ \dfrac{7}{13}$

16. $\dfrac{2}{7}$
    $+ \dfrac{1}{5}$

17. $\dfrac{4}{5}$
    $+ \dfrac{3}{6}$

18. $\dfrac{2}{7}$
    $+ \dfrac{1}{3}$

19. $\dfrac{4}{8}$
    $+ \dfrac{3}{7}$

20. $\dfrac{1}{2}$
    $+ \dfrac{3}{4}$

Total Problems __20__ Problems Correct ____

Name_____   Skill: Adding Fractions with Different
                                              Denominators

Add and write the answers in simplest form.

1. $\dfrac{2}{5}$
    $+\dfrac{1}{2}$

2. $\dfrac{3}{10}$
    $+\dfrac{1}{3}$

3. $\dfrac{7}{8}$
    $+\dfrac{1}{3}$

4. $\dfrac{2}{10}$
    $+\dfrac{3}{4}$

5. $\dfrac{2}{3}$
    $+\dfrac{4}{5}$

6. $\dfrac{2}{3}$
    $+\dfrac{3}{4}$

7. $\dfrac{1}{3}$
    $+\dfrac{2}{5}$

8. $\dfrac{5}{6}$
    $+\dfrac{2}{5}$

9. $\dfrac{5}{6}$
    $+\dfrac{1}{4}$

10. $\dfrac{3}{12}$
    $+\dfrac{2}{4}$

11. $\dfrac{6}{12}$
    $+\dfrac{3}{10}$

12. $\dfrac{2}{6}$
    $+\dfrac{5}{12}$

13. $\dfrac{1}{7}$
    $+\dfrac{5}{8}$

14. $\dfrac{1}{4}$
    $+\dfrac{2}{5}$

15. $\dfrac{5}{13}$
    $+\dfrac{7}{12}$

16. $\dfrac{2}{6}$
    $+\dfrac{1}{8}$

17. $\dfrac{4}{8}$
    $+\dfrac{3}{5}$

18. $\dfrac{2}{9}$
    $+\dfrac{2}{3}$

19. $\dfrac{2}{4}$
    $+\dfrac{3}{7}$

20. $\dfrac{1}{3}$
    $+\dfrac{3}{6}$

Total Problems 20   Problems Correct ____

48

Name_____

Add and write the answers in simplest form.

1. $4\frac{5}{8}$
$+\ 3\frac{1}{6}$

2. $3\frac{2}{5}$
$+\ 2\frac{1}{2}$

3. $1\frac{7}{9}$
$+\ 4\frac{1}{5}$

4. $6\frac{3}{10}$
$+\ 7\frac{1}{3}$

5. $2\frac{5}{6}$
$+\ 6\frac{3}{4}$

6. $8\frac{5}{7}$
$+\ 9\frac{2}{3}$

7. $6\frac{5}{6}$
$+\ 2\frac{2}{3}$

8. $5\frac{4}{5}$
$+\ 3\frac{2}{3}$

9. $4\frac{5}{8}$
$+\ 5\frac{4}{12}$

10. $8\frac{2}{3}$
$+\ 1\frac{5}{9}$

11. $4\frac{2}{14}$
$+\ 6\frac{3}{7}$

12. $3\frac{1}{6}$
$+\ 4\frac{2}{3}$

13. $10\frac{3}{8}$
$+\ 3\frac{1}{2}$

14. $2\frac{3}{4}$
$+\ 7\frac{1}{2}$

15. $1\frac{1}{4}$
$+\ 5\frac{10}{12}$

16. $9\frac{1}{2}$
$+\ 8\frac{3}{7}$

Total Problems _16_ Problems Correct ____

Name_____

Add and write the answers in simplest form.

1. $1\frac{3}{8}$
    $+\ 2\frac{1}{2}$

2. $5\frac{2}{5}$
    $+\ 3\frac{1}{3}$

3. $5\frac{3}{4}$
    $+\ 6\frac{5}{6}$

4. $4\frac{7}{12}$
    $+\ 5\frac{1}{2}$

5. $3\frac{11}{12}$
    $+\ 4\frac{1}{2}$

6. $2\frac{4}{9}$
    $+\ 5\frac{1}{3}$

7. $1\frac{3}{4}$
    $+\ 3\frac{2}{3}$

8. $10\frac{5}{8}$
    $+\ 2\frac{2}{3}$

9. $6\frac{5}{6}$
    $+\ 4\frac{2}{3}$

10. $2\frac{2}{7}$
    $+\ 1\frac{1}{3}$

11. $4\frac{3}{5}$
    $+\ 5\frac{1}{4}$

12. $12\frac{3}{4}$
    $+\ 8\frac{2}{5}$

13. $7\frac{2}{3}$
    $+\ 8\frac{4}{5}$

14. $2\frac{7}{8}$
    $+\ 4\frac{5}{6}$

15. $1\frac{5}{7}$
    $+\ 4\frac{3}{12}$

16. $9\frac{1}{8}$
    $+\ 6\frac{3}{4}$

Total Problems __16__ Problems Correct ____

50

Add and write the answers in simplest form.

1. $2\frac{1}{3} + 4\frac{1}{3} =$ 2. $6\frac{1}{9} + 3\frac{2}{9} =$ 3. $1\frac{1}{6} + 2\frac{3}{8} =$

4. $2\frac{3}{4} + 7\frac{1}{3} =$ 5. $1\frac{3}{8} + 2\frac{1}{3} =$ 6. $4\frac{10}{12} + 6\frac{11}{15} =$

7. $\frac{1}{8} + \frac{1}{4} =$ 8. $\frac{2}{5} + \frac{1}{5} =$ 9. $\frac{3}{3} + \frac{1}{7} =$ 10. $\frac{1}{2} + \frac{2}{3} =$

11. $\frac{3}{7} + \frac{1}{2} =$ 12. $\frac{4}{7} + \frac{1}{7} =$ 13. $\frac{3}{9} + \frac{2}{5} =$ 14. $\frac{4}{6} + \frac{2}{6} =$

15. $\frac{2}{9} + \frac{2}{7} =$ 16. $\frac{5}{7} + \frac{2}{6} =$ 17. $\frac{4}{9} + \frac{9}{9} =$ 18. $\frac{2}{3} + \frac{1}{5} =$

Total Problems 18 Problems Correct ____

Name_____

Add and write the answers in simplest form.

1.
$$\frac{2}{3}$$
$$+ \frac{1}{5}$$

2.
$$\frac{2}{10}$$
$$+ \frac{3}{5}$$

3.
$$\frac{2}{7}$$
$$+ \frac{5}{7}$$

4.
$$\frac{3}{11}$$
$$+ \frac{4}{8}$$

5.
$$\frac{3}{4}$$
$$+ \frac{1}{4}$$

6.
$$\frac{4}{5}$$
$$+ \frac{7}{8}$$

7.
$$\frac{1}{10}$$
$$+ \frac{3}{5}$$

8.
$$\frac{4}{5}$$
$$+ \frac{1}{8}$$

9.
$$\frac{2}{7}$$
$$+ \frac{1}{9}$$

10.
$$\frac{2}{12}$$
$$+ \frac{1}{8}$$

11.
$$8\frac{1}{3}$$
$$+ 1\frac{1}{3}$$

12.
$$2\frac{4}{8}$$
$$+ 6\frac{5}{6}$$

13.
$$4\frac{2}{7}$$
$$+ 6\frac{3}{7}$$

14.
$$2\frac{1}{3}$$
$$+ 4\frac{2}{5}$$

15.
$$11\frac{2}{3}$$
$$+ 9\frac{1}{5}$$

16.
$$3\frac{1}{6}$$
$$+ 2\frac{3}{6}$$

17.
$$8\frac{3}{10}$$
$$+ 3\frac{10}{11}$$

18.
$$1\frac{4}{6}$$
$$+ 5\frac{3}{6}$$

Total Problems 18 Problems Correct ____

52

Name_____

Subtract the fractions and write the answers in simplest form.

1. $\dfrac{5}{6}$
    $-\dfrac{1}{6}$

2. $\dfrac{7}{8}$
    $-\dfrac{3}{8}$

3. $\dfrac{3}{10}$
    $-\dfrac{1}{10}$

4. $\dfrac{15}{16}$
    $-\dfrac{11}{16}$

5. $\dfrac{3}{4}$
    $-\dfrac{1}{4}$

6. $\dfrac{7}{12}$
    $-\dfrac{5}{12}$

7. $\dfrac{5}{7}$
    $-\dfrac{2}{7}$

8. $\dfrac{7}{9}$
    $-\dfrac{1}{9}$

9. $\dfrac{4}{5}$
    $-\dfrac{2}{5}$

10. $\dfrac{13}{15}$
    $-\dfrac{11}{15}$

11. $\dfrac{9}{14}$
    $-\dfrac{1}{14}$

12. $\dfrac{9}{11}$
    $-\dfrac{1}{11}$

13. $\dfrac{5}{8}$
    $-\dfrac{1}{8}$

14. $\dfrac{2}{3}$
    $-\dfrac{1}{3}$

15. $\dfrac{9}{10}$
    $-\dfrac{7}{10}$

16. $\dfrac{7}{8}$
    $-\dfrac{5}{8}$

17. $\dfrac{5}{9}$
    $-\dfrac{4}{9}$

18. $\dfrac{5}{7}$
    $-\dfrac{3}{7}$

19. $\dfrac{2}{5}$
    $-\dfrac{1}{5}$

20. $\dfrac{3}{3}$
    $-\dfrac{1}{3}$

Total Problems 20 Problems Correct ____

Name_____

Subtract the fractions and write the answers in simplest form.

1. $\dfrac{2}{5} - \dfrac{1}{5} =$

2. $\dfrac{7}{9} - \dfrac{3}{9} =$

3. $\dfrac{3}{8} - \dfrac{2}{8} =$

4. $\dfrac{5}{9} - \dfrac{2}{9} =$

5. $\dfrac{5}{10} - \dfrac{2}{10} =$

6. $\dfrac{2}{3} - \dfrac{1}{3} =$

7. $\dfrac{6}{7} - \dfrac{1}{7} =$

8. $\dfrac{5}{5} - \dfrac{2}{5} =$

9. $\dfrac{3}{4} - \dfrac{2}{4} =$

10. $\dfrac{5}{6} - \dfrac{3}{6} =$

11. $\dfrac{9}{20} - \dfrac{2}{20} =$

12. $\dfrac{1}{7} - \dfrac{1}{7} =$

13. $\dfrac{2}{9} - \dfrac{2}{9} =$

14. $\dfrac{2}{2} - \dfrac{1}{2} =$

15. $\dfrac{1}{1} - \dfrac{1}{1} =$

Total Problems __15__ Problems Correct ____

Name_____

Subtract and write the answers in simplest form.

1.
$$2 - \frac{7}{8}$$

2.
$$4 - \frac{3}{5}$$

3.
$$3 - \frac{3}{4}$$

4.
$$8 - \frac{9}{9}$$

5.
$$7 - \frac{4}{5}$$

6.
$$4 - \frac{3}{10}$$

7.
$$5 - \frac{6}{9}$$

8.
$$4 - \frac{3}{6}$$

9.
$$5 - \frac{2}{5}$$

10.
$$10 - \frac{1}{2}$$

11.
$$12 - \frac{5}{7}$$

12.
$$9 - \frac{1}{3}$$

13.
$$4 - \frac{7}{8}$$

14.
$$3 - \frac{6}{7}$$

15.
$$6 - \frac{1}{6}$$

16.
$$5 - \frac{1}{4}$$

17.
$$4 - \frac{2}{6}$$

18.
$$3 - \frac{2}{3}$$

19.
$$2 - \frac{6}{8}$$

20.
$$1 - \frac{3}{5}$$

Total Problems __20__ Problems Correct ____

55

Name_____

Subtract the fractions and write the answers in simplest form.

1.
$$15 - \frac{3}{8}$$

2.
$$10 - \frac{2}{5}$$

3.
$$1 - \frac{1}{3}$$

4.
$$2 - \frac{6}{11}$$

5.
$$5 - \frac{3}{5}$$

6.
$$9 - \frac{3}{11}$$

7.
$$14 - \frac{2}{9}$$

8.
$$13 - \frac{2}{3}$$

9.
$$1 - \frac{7}{8}$$

10.
$$10 - \frac{1}{3}$$

11.
$$12 - \frac{3}{5}$$

12.
$$6 - \frac{1}{5}$$

13.
$$7 - \frac{5}{6}$$

14.
$$5 - \frac{1}{4}$$

15.
$$8 - \frac{3}{4}$$

16.
$$4 - \frac{1}{2}$$

17.
$$2 - \frac{1}{6}$$

18.
$$2 - \frac{4}{5}$$

19.
$$6 - \frac{6}{9}$$

20.
$$7 - \frac{3}{7}$$

Total Problems 20 Problems Correct ____

Name_____

Subtract and write the answers in simplest form.

1. $5\frac{5}{8}$
   $-\ 2\frac{4}{8}$
   _____

2. $8\frac{4}{5}$
   $-\ 4\frac{1}{5}$
   _____

3. $5\frac{2}{3}$
   $-\ 1\frac{1}{3}$
   _____

4. $3\frac{2}{10}$
   $-\ 1\frac{2}{10}$
   _____

5. $4\frac{2}{6}$
   $-\ 3\frac{5}{6}$
   _____

6. $3\frac{2}{6}$
   $-\ 2\frac{1}{6}$
   _____

7. $10\frac{3}{4}$
   $-\ 7\frac{1}{4}$
   _____

8. $6\frac{7}{8}$
   $-\ 1\frac{1}{8}$
   _____

9. $5\frac{5}{8}$
   $-\ 3\frac{4}{8}$
   _____

10. $9\frac{6}{7}$
    $-\ 2\frac{2}{7}$
    _____

11. $5\frac{3}{3}$
    $-\ 4\frac{2}{3}$
    _____

12. $2\frac{1}{8}$
    $-\ 1\frac{1}{8}$
    _____

13. $7\frac{3}{5}$
    $-\ 5\frac{1}{5}$
    _____

14. $8\frac{7}{9}$
    $-\ 8\frac{6}{9}$
    _____

15. $4\frac{9}{10}$
    $-\ 2\frac{7}{10}$
    _____

16. $2\frac{3}{5}$
    $-\ 1\frac{4}{5}$
    _____

Total Problems __16__ **Problems Correct** _____

Name_____

Subtract and write the answers in simplest form.

1. $12\frac{7}{8}$
$-\ 5\frac{5}{8}$

2. $10\frac{2}{5}$
$-\ 7\frac{4}{5}$

3. $5\frac{2}{3}$
$-\ 1\frac{1}{3}$

4. $6\frac{2}{12}$
$-\ 3\frac{2}{12}$

5. $2\frac{2}{3}$
$-\ 2\frac{1}{3}$

6. $3\frac{1}{4}$
$-\ 2\frac{3}{4}$

7. $8\frac{7}{10}$
$-\ 7\frac{9}{10}$

8. $4\frac{5}{6}$
$-\ 2\frac{1}{6}$

9. $9\frac{7}{8}$
$-\ 4\frac{4}{8}$

10. $10\frac{2}{3}$
$-\ 9\frac{1}{3}$

11. $8\frac{3}{16}$
$-\ 7\frac{5}{16}$

12. $4\frac{11}{18}$
$-\ 1\frac{7}{18}$

13. $3\frac{1}{8}$
$-\ 1\frac{7}{8}$

14. $5\frac{4}{5}$
$-\ 4\frac{1}{5}$

15. $6\frac{7}{15}$
$-\ 2\frac{8}{15}$

16. $8\frac{7}{10}$
$-\ 1\frac{3}{10}$

Total Problems 16   Problems Correct ____

Name_____

Skill: Subtracting Fractions with Different Denominators

Subtract the fractions and write the answers in simplest form.

1. $\dfrac{1}{3}$
    $-\dfrac{1}{4}$

2. $\dfrac{3}{5}$
    $-\dfrac{1}{3}$

3. $\dfrac{7}{12}$
    $-\dfrac{1}{4}$

4. $\dfrac{2}{3}$
    $-\dfrac{1}{2}$

5. $\dfrac{5}{6}$
    $-\dfrac{1}{5}$

6. $\dfrac{3}{4}$
    $-\dfrac{1}{5}$

7. $\dfrac{3}{8}$
    $-\dfrac{2}{6}$

8. $\dfrac{3}{9}$
    $-\dfrac{1}{4}$

9. $\dfrac{2}{3}$
    $-\dfrac{4}{9}$

10. $\dfrac{7}{8}$
    $-\dfrac{3}{10}$

11. $\dfrac{9}{10}$
    $-\dfrac{5}{7}$

12. $\dfrac{2}{4}$
    $-\dfrac{1}{3}$

13. $\dfrac{7}{8}$
    $-\dfrac{1}{9}$

14. $\dfrac{1}{3}$
    $-\dfrac{1}{6}$

15. $\dfrac{9}{12}$
    $-\dfrac{2}{11}$

16. $\dfrac{5}{7}$
    $-\dfrac{2}{9}$

17. $\dfrac{1}{5}$
    $-\dfrac{1}{8}$

18. $\dfrac{8}{8}$
    $-\dfrac{4}{6}$

19. $\dfrac{8}{9}$
    $-\dfrac{3}{6}$

20. $\dfrac{6}{6}$
    $-\dfrac{3}{12}$

Total Problems 20   Problems Correct ____

Name_____

Subtract the fractions and write the answers in simplest form.

1. $\dfrac{3}{4}$
   $-\dfrac{1}{6}$

2. $\dfrac{5}{6}$
   $-\dfrac{2}{5}$

3. $\dfrac{11}{12}$
   $-\dfrac{1}{6}$

4. $\dfrac{5}{12}$
   $-\dfrac{1}{3}$

5. $\dfrac{3}{4}$
   $-\dfrac{1}{3}$

6. $\dfrac{13}{15}$
   $-\dfrac{2}{3}$

7. $\dfrac{2}{3}$
   $-\dfrac{1}{6}$

8. $\dfrac{5}{6}$
   $-\dfrac{3}{7}$

9. $\dfrac{7}{8}$
   $-\dfrac{1}{6}$

10. $\dfrac{8}{9}$
    $-\dfrac{5}{6}$

11. $\dfrac{2}{3}$
    $-\dfrac{7}{12}$

12. $\dfrac{11}{14}$
    $-\dfrac{1}{2}$

13. $\dfrac{7}{8}$
    $-\dfrac{1}{9}$

14. $\dfrac{1}{3}$
    $-\dfrac{1}{6}$

15. $\dfrac{9}{12}$
    $-\dfrac{2}{11}$

16. $\dfrac{5}{6}$
    $-\dfrac{1}{3}$

17. $\dfrac{7}{12}$
    $-\dfrac{1}{4}$

18. $\dfrac{7}{8}$
    $-\dfrac{1}{2}$

19. $\dfrac{2}{3}$
    $-\dfrac{4}{9}$

20. $\dfrac{5}{6}$
    $-\dfrac{1}{8}$

Total Problems 20   Problems Correct ____

Name_____

Subtract and write the answers in simplest form.

1. $2\frac{2}{3}$
$- 1\frac{1}{2}$

2. $4\frac{7}{10}$
$- 1\frac{2}{5}$

3. $4\frac{1}{3}$
$- 1\frac{2}{5}$

4. $6\frac{2}{7}$
$- 4\frac{1}{2}$

5. $4\frac{1}{3}$
$- 2\frac{3}{8}$

6. $3\frac{7}{8}$
$- 2\frac{1}{6}$

7. $5\frac{5}{12}$
$- 3\frac{7}{10}$

8. $4\frac{2}{5}$
$- 2\frac{3}{10}$

9. $3\frac{5}{6}$
$- 2\frac{1}{12}$

10. $5\frac{4}{9}$
$- 2\frac{1}{3}$

11. $3\frac{5}{6}$
$- 1\frac{5}{9}$

12. $6\frac{4}{5}$
$- 5\frac{3}{7}$

13. $5\frac{5}{8}$
$- 2\frac{3}{4}$

14. $3\frac{1}{2}$
$- 1\frac{3}{4}$

15. $7\frac{3}{5}$
$- 4\frac{7}{10}$

16. $4\frac{7}{8}$
$- 2\frac{1}{4}$

Total Problems __16__ Problems Correct ____

Name_____

Subtract and write the answers in simplest form.

1.
$$5 \frac{1}{6}$$
$$- \ 2 \frac{3}{4}$$

2.
$$4 \frac{1}{3}$$
$$- \ 1 \frac{1}{4}$$

3.
$$6 \frac{1}{2}$$
$$- \ 1 \frac{1}{3}$$

4.
$$5 \frac{1}{3}$$
$$- \ 3 \frac{3}{4}$$

5.
$$4 \frac{7}{10}$$
$$- \ 1 \frac{4}{5}$$

6.
$$3 \frac{7}{12}$$
$$- \ 1 \frac{9}{10}$$

7.
$$7 \frac{1}{4}$$
$$- \ 3 \frac{2}{3}$$

8.
$$8 \frac{2}{5}$$
$$- \ 4 \frac{1}{4}$$

9.
$$5 \frac{7}{8}$$
$$- \ 1 \frac{1}{16}$$

10.
$$5 \frac{4}{5}$$
$$- \ 2 \frac{1}{3}$$

11.
$$10 \frac{4}{5}$$
$$- \ 6 \frac{5}{6}$$

12.
$$2 \frac{2}{3}$$
$$- \ 2 \frac{1}{4}$$

13.
$$3 \frac{1}{3}$$
$$- \ 1 \frac{5}{6}$$

14.
$$4 \frac{3}{4}$$
$$- \ 1 \frac{5}{6}$$

15.
$$12 \frac{2}{3}$$
$$- \ 9 \frac{6}{7}$$

16.
$$6 \frac{1}{3}$$
$$- \ 5 \frac{3}{4}$$

Total Problems __16__ Problems Correct ____

Multiply the fractions and write answers in simplest form.

1. $\dfrac{3}{4}$ x $\dfrac{2}{5}$ =

2. $\dfrac{1}{4}$ x $\dfrac{3}{5}$ =

3. $\dfrac{1}{8}$ x $\dfrac{2}{5}$ =

4. $\dfrac{7}{8}$ x $\dfrac{1}{6}$ =

5. $\dfrac{4}{7}$ x $\dfrac{3}{8}$ =

6. $\dfrac{1}{6}$ x $\dfrac{2}{3}$ =

7. $\dfrac{4}{5}$ x $\dfrac{2}{3}$ =

8. $\dfrac{2}{3}$ x $\dfrac{2}{5}$ =

9. $\dfrac{1}{2}$ x $\dfrac{3}{4}$ =

10. $\dfrac{1}{3}$ x $\dfrac{1}{5}$ =

11. $\dfrac{2}{3}$ x $\dfrac{4}{5}$ =

12. $\dfrac{1}{8}$ x $\dfrac{1}{3}$ =

13. $\dfrac{2}{7}$ x $\dfrac{2}{9}$ =

14. $\dfrac{3}{5}$ x $\dfrac{1}{3}$ =

15. $\dfrac{1}{6}$ x $\dfrac{4}{5}$ =

Total Problems __15__ Problems Correct _____

Multiply the fractions and write answers in simplest form.

1. $\dfrac{1}{3}$ x $\dfrac{1}{7}$ =

2. $\dfrac{1}{4}$ x $\dfrac{1}{6}$ =

3. $\dfrac{1}{5}$ x $\dfrac{5}{6}$ =

4. $\dfrac{3}{5}$ x $\dfrac{2}{9}$ =

5. $\dfrac{2}{3}$ x $\dfrac{3}{8}$ =

6. $\dfrac{1}{2}$ x $\dfrac{3}{7}$ =

7. $\dfrac{1}{6}$ x $\dfrac{4}{5}$ =

8. $\dfrac{3}{4}$ x $\dfrac{4}{7}$ =

9. $\dfrac{2}{5}$ x $\dfrac{4}{9}$ =

10. $\dfrac{2}{7}$ x $\dfrac{5}{8}$ =

11. $\dfrac{2}{5}$ x $\dfrac{5}{6}$ =

12. $\dfrac{2}{8}$ x $\dfrac{3}{3}$ =

13. $\dfrac{2}{5}$ x $\dfrac{4}{9}$ =

14. $\dfrac{4}{5}$ x $\dfrac{2}{3}$ =

15. $\dfrac{1}{7}$ x $\dfrac{6}{8}$ =

Total Problems _15_ Problems Correct ____

Name_____

Multiply and write the answers in simplest form.

1. $4 \times \frac{1}{2} =$

2. $\frac{2}{5} \times 3 =$

3. $\frac{1}{3} \times 7 =$

4. $2 \times \frac{2}{5} =$

5. $\frac{1}{8} \times 5 =$

6. $4 \times \frac{3}{4} =$

7. $4 \times \frac{2}{7} =$

8. $\frac{5}{7} \times 5 =$

9. $\frac{6}{8} \times 2 =$

10. $3 \times \frac{5}{6} =$

11. $\frac{2}{3} \times 2 =$

12. $5 \times \frac{4}{5} =$

13. $8 \times \frac{1}{8} =$

14. $\frac{3}{9} \times 4 =$

15. $3 \times \frac{2}{3} =$

Total Problems 15 Problems Correct ____

Multiply and write the answers in simplest form.

1. $5 \times \dfrac{2}{5} =$

2. $\dfrac{2}{3} \times 4 =$

3. $\dfrac{3}{4} \times 5 =$

4. $8 \times \dfrac{1}{7} =$

5. $\dfrac{1}{9} \times 6 =$

6. $2 \times \dfrac{4}{5} =$

7. $6 \times \dfrac{3}{8} =$

8. $\dfrac{5}{6} \times 4 =$

9. $\dfrac{2}{7} \times 6 =$

10. $4 \times \dfrac{8}{9} =$

11. $\dfrac{4}{6} \times 3 =$

12. $7 \times \dfrac{3}{5} =$

13. $2 \times \dfrac{3}{7} =$

14. $\dfrac{4}{5} \times 6 =$

15. $7 \times \dfrac{5}{6} =$

Total Problems __15__ Problems Correct ____

Name_____

Multiply and write the answers in simplest form.

1. $10 \times \dfrac{2}{3} =$

2. $9 \times \dfrac{5}{6} =$

3. $12 \times \dfrac{7}{8} =$

4. $4 \times \dfrac{4}{7} =$

5. $3 \times \dfrac{1}{3} =$

6. $5 \times \dfrac{3}{4} =$

7. $7 \times \dfrac{10}{11} =$

8. $30 \times \dfrac{3}{90} =$

9. $22 \times \dfrac{1}{44} =$

10. $36 \times \dfrac{2}{288} =$

11. $12 \times \dfrac{1}{36} =$

12. $4 \times \dfrac{1}{8} =$

13. $6 \times \dfrac{4}{8} =$

14. $5 \times \dfrac{2}{5} =$

15. $8 \times \dfrac{2}{3} =$

Total Problems __15__ Problems Correct ____

Name_____ Skill: Multiplying Mixed Numbers
                                       and Whole Numbers

Multiply and write the answers in simplest form.

1. $2 \times 2\frac{1}{3} =$ 2. $4 \times 5\frac{1}{8} =$ 3. $7 \times 1\frac{3}{4} =$

4. $3 \times 5\frac{1}{5} =$ 5. $6 \times 3\frac{1}{6} =$ 6. $7 \times 2\frac{3}{5} =$

7. $9 \times 3\frac{2}{3} =$ 8. $5 \times 6\frac{5}{8} =$ 9. $4 \times 2\frac{1}{2} =$

10. $8 \times 9\frac{1}{10} =$ 11. $3 \times 9\frac{1}{3} =$ 12. $7 \times 2\frac{1}{7} =$

Total Problems 12 Problems Correct ____

68

Name_____

Multiply and write the answers in simplest form.

1. $4 \times 3\frac{3}{5} =$

2. $10 \times 5\frac{1}{2} =$

3. $2 \times 5\frac{1}{8} =$

4. $6 \times 9\frac{4}{5} =$

5. $8 \times 2\frac{3}{8} =$

6. $3 \times 1\frac{15}{16} =$

7. $2 \times 8\frac{3}{4} =$

8. $5 \times 4\frac{2}{5} =$

9. $4 \times 8\frac{6}{7} =$

10. $9 \times 1\frac{1}{18} =$

11. $2 \times 7\frac{5}{8} =$

12. $2 \times 2\frac{1}{4} =$

Total Problems 12   Problems Correct ____

Name_____ Skill: Multiplying Mixed Numbers

Multiply and write the answers in simplest form.

1. $3\frac{1}{2} \times 2\frac{1}{2} =$

2. $2\frac{2}{3} \times 4\frac{2}{5} =$

3. $6\frac{7}{8} \times 3\frac{1}{3} =$

4. $8\frac{5}{6} \times 3\frac{6}{7} =$

5. $5\frac{3}{4} \times 6\frac{1}{4} =$

6. $7\frac{9}{10} \times 8\frac{7}{8} =$

7. $4\frac{2}{5} \times 6\frac{2}{3} =$

8. $2\frac{8}{9} \times 7\frac{7}{8} =$

9. $4\frac{1}{4} \times 3\frac{5}{6} =$

10. $4\frac{2}{9} \times 5\frac{10}{11} =$

11. $7\frac{1}{4} \times 3\frac{3}{7} =$

12. $8\frac{3}{5} \times 1\frac{1}{2} =$

Total Problems   12   Problems Correct ____

Name_____   Skill: Multiplying Mixed Numbers

Multiply and write the answers in simplest form.

1. $8\frac{1}{4} \times 6\frac{2}{3} =$

2. $5\frac{1}{5} \times 4\frac{1}{3} =$

3. $7\frac{2}{5} \times 9\frac{1}{8} =$

4. $9\frac{9}{10} \times 4\frac{7}{8} =$

5. $2\frac{5}{6} \times 12\frac{4}{5} =$

6. $1\frac{10}{13} \times 2\frac{9}{13} =$

7. $4\frac{2}{7} \times 6\frac{1}{10} =$

8. $8\frac{3}{5} \times 4\frac{5}{6} =$

Total Problems 8   Problems Correct ____

Name_____

Add.

1. 14.2
  + 12.1

2. 12.3
  + 15.2

3. 18.2
  + 16.5

4. 22.2
  + 13.1

5. 47.5
  + 32.6

6. 54.8
  + 13.2

7. 18.7
  + 10.5

8. 16.6
  + 13.8

9. 15.2
  + 13.0

10. 12.0
  + 14.9

11. 49.4
  + 11.1

12. 34.2
  + 17.2

13. 1.47
  + 6.54

14. 7.85
  + 9.41

15. 2.22
  + 3.94

16. 7.54
  + 2.24

17. 8.85
  + 7.33

18. 12.95 + 5.06 = _____

19. 16.3 + 35.7 = _____

20. 13.8 + 6.9 = _____

21. 3.25 + 3.25 = _____

22. 46.02 + 75.67 = _____

23. 87.01 + 16.53 = _____

Total Problems __23__ Problems Correct ____

Skill: Adding Decimals

Add.

1.
```
   4.15
   6.20
 + 8.63
```

2.
```
   2.26
   3.43
 + 8.15
```

3.
```
  32.15
  64.23
 + 32.57
```

4.
```
   3.564
   1.508
 + 1.521
```

5.
```
   8.461
    .003
 +  .212
```

6.
```
    .491
    .320
 +  .617
```

7.
```
  14.501
  62.037
 + 8.693
```

8.
```
  62.715
   1.307
 +  .032
```

9.
```
   7.35
  33.421
 + 42.6
```

10.
```
   1.908
    .076
 + 22.444
```

11.
```
    .179
   2.602
 + 62.561
```

12.
```
   7.35
  16.201
 + 2.9
```

13. 8.16 + 15.204 + 35.8 = _____

14. .007 + 1.12 + 5.978 = _____

Total Problems __14__ Problems Correct _____

73

Name_____

Subtract.

1. 5.6
  − 3.2

2. 7.8
  − 4.5

3. 6.3
  − 4.1

4. 8.6
  − 5.2

5. 7.6
  − 3.2

6. 10.4
  − 8.2

7. 9.3
  − 7.5

8. 8.7
  − 5.2

9. 16.4
  − 8.2

10. 26.7
  − 2.5

11. 8.5
  − 3.5

12. 86.5
  − 2.3

13. 9.65
  − 4.22

14. 75.4
  − 3.1

15. 16.2
  − 4.1

16. 72.5 − 63.7 = _____

17. 8.1 − 6.5 = _____

Total Problems 17 Problems Correct ____

Name_____ Skill: Subtracting Decimals

Subtract.

1. 326.7   2. 1.589   3. 52.07   4. 8.123   5. 1.978
  − 42.8   − .756   − 3.9   − 6.017   − 1.682

6. 14.021   7. 16.882   8. 7.57   9. 18.9   10. 14.9
  − 5.6   − 9.3   − 6.85   − 16.425   − 3.2

11. 19.5 − .001 = _____   12. 28.4 − 4.62 = _____

13. .501 − .332 = _____   14. 33.45 − 15.4 = _____

15. 42.642 − 10.35 = _____   16. 18.5 − 9.5 = _____

Total Problems __16__ Problems Correct ____

Name_____

Multiply.

1. 5.2
    x 1.8

2. 2.2
    x 4.4

3. 1.3
    x 1.0

4. 6.4
    x 2.5

5. 5.4
    x 1.3

6. 10.5
    x 6.6

7. .12
    x 3.7

8. 7.1
    x .25

9. 16.2
    x 1.1

10. 6.6
    x 1.5

11. 2.8
    x 9.9

12. 5.20
    x .21

13. 7.54
    x 2.77

14. 2.0
    x 2.1

15. 4.44
    x .01

16. .34 x .12 = _____

17. 6.1 x 2.5 = _____

18. 45.5 x 4.6 = _____

19. 5.6 x 7.3 = _____

Total Problems _19_ Problems Correct ____

Name_____

Divide.

1. $2\overline{)8.44}$ 　　2. $7\overline{)3.92}$ 　　3. $6\overline{)3.6}$ 　　4. $4\overline{)9.6}$

5. $5\overline{)1.25}$ 　　6. $2\overline{)9.4}$ 　　7. $7\overline{)3.92}$ 　　8. $5\overline{).865}$

9. $14\overline{)1.218}$ 　10. $24\overline{)17.28}$ 　11. $46\overline{).2346}$ 　12. $67\overline{)274.7}$

13. $38.6 \div 2 =$ _____　　　14. $42.3 \div 3 =$ _____

15. $.6566 \div 67 =$ _____　　16. $.7255 \div 5 =$ _____

17. $166.4 \div 52 =$ _____　　18. $166.0 \div 10 =$ _____

Total Problems _18_ Problems Correct ____

Divide.

1. $.8\overline{)64}$ 2. $.5\overline{)35}$ 3. $.3\overline{)9}$ 4. $.12\overline{)360}$

5. $.25\overline{)100}$ 6. $1.2\overline{)48}$ 7. $9.6\overline{)82.8}$ 8. $.23\overline{)2.185}$

9. $6.1\overline{)7.93}$ 10. $5.3\overline{)42.4}$ 11. $.17\overline{)3.23}$ 12. $7.2\overline{)40.32}$

13. $64 \div .4 =$ _____   14. $152 \div .8 =$ _____

15. $4.9 \div .7 =$ _____   16. $.63 \div .3 =$ _____

17. $15.2 \div .19 =$ _____   18. $1.365 \div 2.1 =$ _____

Total Problems 18 Problems Correct ____

Name_____   Skill: Changing Decimals to Fractions

Change each decimal to a fraction. Write your answer in simplest form.

1. .5 = _____   2. .1 = _____   3. .4 = _____

4. .6 = _____   5. .2 = _____   6. .8 = _____

7. .7 = _____   8. 4.1 = _____   9. 5.2 = _____

10. 9.5 = _____   11. 3.6 = _____   12. 2.5 = _____

13. 1.8 = _____   14. 7.3 = _____   15. 6.5 = _____

16. 2.2 = _____   17. 3.9 = _____   18. 4.2 = _____

19. 6.2 = _____   20. 8.8 = _____   21. 4.1 = _____

22. 1.25 = _____   23. 2.50 = _____   24. 9.3 = _____

Total Problems _24_ Problems Correct ____

Name_____ Skill: Changing Decimals to Fractions

Change each decimal to a fraction. Write your answer in simplest form.

1. **8.2** = _____

2. **9.1** = _____

3. **7.6** = _____

4. **5.4** = _____

5. **10.6** = _____

6. **25.3** = _____

7. **48.2** = _____

8. **.25** = _____

9. **.75** = _____

10. **.15** = _____

11. **.68** = _____

12. **4.36** = _____

13. **25.32** = _____

14. **86.12** = _____

15. **9.45** = _____

16. **3.25** = _____

17. **6.5** = _____

18. **75.2** = _____

19. **30.2** = _____

20. **9.12** = _____

21. **25.2** = _____

22. **.625** = _____

23. **.125** = _____

24. **25.0** = _____

Total Problems __24__ Problems Correct ____

Name_____ Skill: Changing Fractions to Decimals

Change the fractions to decimals. Round to the nearest thousandth when necessary.

1. $\dfrac{5}{8}$ = _____

2. $\dfrac{1}{4}$ = _____

3. $\dfrac{3}{4}$ = _____

4. $\dfrac{1}{8}$ = _____

5. $\dfrac{7}{8}$ = _____

6. $\dfrac{5}{6}$ = _____

7. $\dfrac{1}{5}$ = _____

8. $\dfrac{4}{5}$ = _____

9. $\dfrac{9}{10}$ = _____

10. $\dfrac{1}{12}$ = _____

11. $\dfrac{2}{7}$ = _____

12. $\dfrac{11}{20}$ = _____

13. $\dfrac{1}{20}$ = _____

14. $\dfrac{3}{5}$ = _____

15. $\dfrac{1}{6}$ = _____

16. $\dfrac{5}{9}$ = _____

17. $\dfrac{3}{6}$ = _____

18. $\dfrac{8}{8}$ = _____

Total Problems _18_ Problems Correct ____

Name_____   Skill: Changing Fractions to Decimals
                                          and Decimals to Fractions

Complete the chart. Round to the nearest thousandth when necessary.

	Fraction	Decimal
1.	$\frac{1}{4}$	
2.		.125
3.	$\frac{1}{3}$	
4.		.834
5.	$\frac{7}{8}$	
6.		.222
7.	$\frac{9}{10}$	
8.		.2
9.	$\frac{3}{8}$	
10.		.8

Total Problems __10__ Problems Correct ____

Circle the correct name for each of the following.

1.   **Line KL**   **Line Segment KL**   **Line K**

2.   **Line FD**   **Line Segment DF**   **Line DF**

3.   **Line BB**   **Line Segment AB**   **Line AB**

4.   **Line CF**   **Line Segment CF**   **Line FC**

5.   **Line MM**   **Line Segment EM**   **Line EM**

6.   **Line NP**   **Line Segment NP**   **Line PN**

7.   **Line OR**   **Line Segment OR**   **Line RO**

8.   **Line SU**   **Line Segment SU**   **Line S**

9.   **Line V**   **Line Segment VX**   **Line VX**

10. **Line TQ**   **Line Segment TQ**   **Line Q**

Draw and label the following.

11. **Line Segment BR**

12. **Line Segment ST**

13. **Line AB**

Total Problems __13__ Problems Correct _____

Name_____   Skill: Naming Angles

Circle the correct names for the following angles.

1. 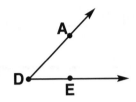 ∠DEA ∠DAE ∠ADE

2. 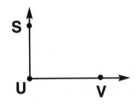 ∠UVS ∠SUV ∠VSS

3. 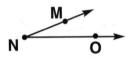 ∠NMO ∠ONM ∠NOM

Name each angle below in the first space. Use a protractor to measure each angle and write the measurement in the second space.

4. 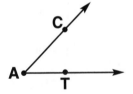 ∠_____ / _____
                              Angle   Degree

5.  ∠_____ / _____
                              Angle   Degree

6.  ∠_____ / _____
                              Angle   Degree

Total Problems 6 Problems Correct ____

Name_____   Skill: Naming Polygons

Write the number of sides of each shape.

1. Triangle _____

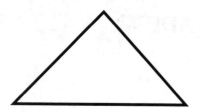

2. Quadrilateral _____

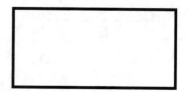

3. Pentagon _____

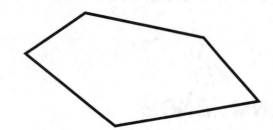

4. Hexagon _____

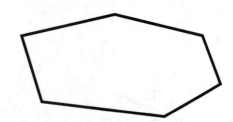

5. Heptagon _____

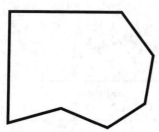

6. Octagon _____

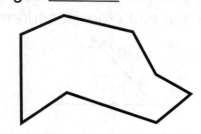

Draw the following.

7. Octagon

8. Pentagon

9. Quadrilateral

10. Heptagon

Total Problems __10__ Problems Correct ____

Name_____

Circle the correct name for the following figures.

1.
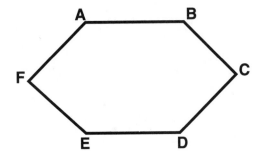

a. Hexagon ABCDEF
b. Hexagon EAFBCD
c. Octagon FCBAED

2.
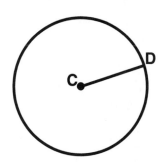

a. Circle A
b. Line Segment A
c. Radius A

3.
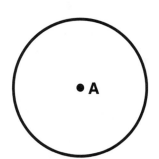

a. Circle D
b. Line Segment A
c. Radius CD

4.   Draw a pentagon and label it RSTUV.

5.   Label the circle according to the instructions.

a. Label the circle – Circle L .
b. Draw a radius. Label it LM.
c. Draw a diameter. Label it NO.

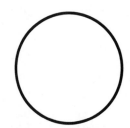

Total Problems __5__ Problems Correct _____

Write the correct abbreviation in the blank.

1. _____ centimeter   m

2. _____ yard   cm

3. _____ foot   mm

4. _____ kilometer   in

5. _____ inch   yd

6. _____ meter   mi

7. _____ mile   ft

8. _____ millimeter   km

Give the equivalents for the following.

9. 1 yd = _____ in   10. 1 m = _____ cm

11. 1 mi = _____ ft   12. 1 cm = _____ m

13. 1 yd = _____ ft   14. 1 km = _____ m

15. 1 mi = _____ yd   16. 1,000 m = _____ km

17. 6 ft = _____ in   18. 5 km = _____ m

19. 3 mi = _____ yd   20. 9 cm = _____ mm

21. 2 yd = _____ in   22. 300 mm = _____ cm

23. 72 in = _____ ft   24. 1 m = _____ km

Total Problems __24__ Problems Correct ____

Name_____

Find the perimeter of each shape.

1. Perimeter = _____ feet

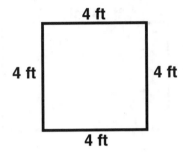

4 ft
4 ft   4 ft
4 ft

2. Perimeter = _____ cm

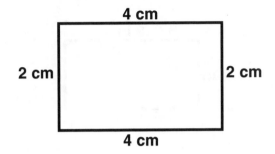

4 cm
2 cm   2 cm
4 cm

3. Perimeter = _____ mm

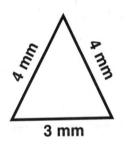

4 mm   4 mm
3 mm

4. Perimeter = _____ mm

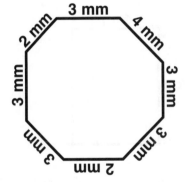

3 mm
2 mm   4 mm
3 mm   3 mm
3 mm   3 mm
2 mm

5. Perimeter = _____ yards

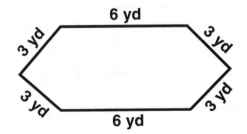

6 yd
3 yd   3 yd
3 yd   3 yd
6 yd

6. Perimeter = _____ km

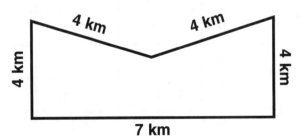

4 km   4 km
4 km   4 km
7 km

Total Problems _6_ Problems Correct ____

Name_____   Skill: Finding Area

Find the area of each shape.

1. Area = _____ square inches

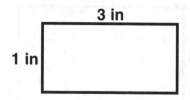

3 in

1 in

2. Area = _____ square miles

4 mi

2 mi

3. Area = _____ square km

4 km

8 km

4. Area = _____ square cm

4 cm

2 cm

Find the area of the quadrilaterals with the following dimensions.

	Length	Width	Area
5.	5 cm	2 cm	square centimeters
6.	10 in	5 in	square inches
7.	4 mi	4 mi	square miles
8.	10 km	2 km	square kilometers
9.	5 ft	3 ft	square feet
10.	4 yd	2 yd	square yards

Total Problems _10_ Problems Correct ____

© Carson-Dellosa CD-3747   **89**

Name_____   Skill: Geometry and Measurement Review

Circle the correct name for each line or line segment.

1. 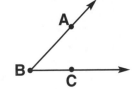   **Line L**   **Line Segment LM**   **Line LM**

2.    **Line NO**   **Line Segment NO**   **Line N**

Write the name of the angle in the first space. Use a protractor to measure it and write the measurement in the second space.

3. 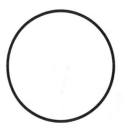   ∠ _____ / _____
                              Angle   Degree

4. Label the circle according to the instructions.

   a. Label the circle – Circle C.
   b. Draw a radius. Label it CD.
   c. Draw a diameter. Label it EF.

5. Write the name of each shape in the blank.

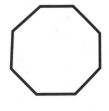 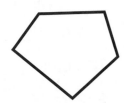  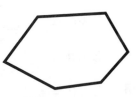

_____   _____   _____   _____

Total Problems __5__ Problems Correct ____

Name_____ Skill: Geometry and Measurement Review

Circle the correct name for the following figures.

1.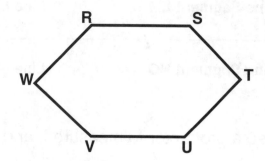

a. **Hexagon RSTUVW**
b. **Octagon RSTUVW**
c. **Octagon RTVX**

2.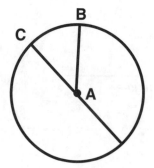

a. **Circle B**
b. **Circle C**
c. **Circle A**

3.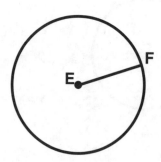

a. **Diameter F**
b. **Radius EF**
c. **Circle G**

Give the equivalents for the following.

4. 2 yd = _____ in

5. 4 m = _____ cm

6. 3 mi = _____ yd

7. 3 cm = _____ m

8. 2 yd = _____ ft

9. 2 km = _____ m

10. 3 ft = _____ yd

11. 11 km = _____ m

12. 3 ft = _____ in

13. 3 m = _____ cm

Total Problems __13__ Problems Correct _____

Add or subtract.

1.   27   2.   86   3.   125   4.   452   5.   865
  + 52   + 75   + 367   − 49   − 72

6.   325   7. 7,254   8.   4,015   9.   6,025   10.   5,094
     415   − 5,132   3,922   4,098   − 2,678
  + 75   + 1,647   + 2,362

Multiply or divide.

11.   92   12.   13   13.   785   14. 14⟌555   15. 37⟌6,721
   x 8   x 63   x 102

16. 63 x 52 = _____   17. 85 x 919 = _____   18. 362 ÷ 12 = _____

Change each fraction to its simplest form.

19. $\dfrac{20}{30}$ =   20. $\dfrac{24}{48}$ =   21. $\dfrac{25}{75}$ =   22. $\dfrac{10}{12}$ =   23. $\dfrac{35}{140}$ =

Change each improper fraction to a mixed number.

24. $\dfrac{8}{6}$ =   25. $\dfrac{25}{10}$ =   26. $\dfrac{51}{15}$ =   27. $\dfrac{16}{9}$ =   28. $\dfrac{120}{18}$ =

Change each mixed number to an improper fraction.

29. $1\dfrac{2}{5}$ =   30. $4\dfrac{3}{8}$ =   31. $3\dfrac{2}{3}$ =   32. $7\dfrac{5}{6}$ =

Total Problems 32   Problems Correct ____

Name_____   Skill: Cumulative Review

Make each pair of fractions equivalent.

1. $\dfrac{1}{3} = \dfrac{}{18}$ 2. $\dfrac{6}{7} = \dfrac{}{42}$ 3. $\dfrac{9}{10} = \dfrac{}{50}$ 4. $\dfrac{3}{4} = \dfrac{}{20}$ 5. $\dfrac{3}{5} = \dfrac{}{25}$

Add or subtract the fractions and mixed numbers. Change to simplest form.

6. $\dfrac{3}{7} + \dfrac{2}{7} =$ 7. $\dfrac{1}{5} + \dfrac{4}{5} =$ 8. $\dfrac{6}{6} + \dfrac{3}{3} =$ 9. $\dfrac{15}{17} + \dfrac{16}{17} =$

10. $4\dfrac{1}{4} - 2\dfrac{3}{4} =$ 11. $3\dfrac{3}{9} + 4\dfrac{5}{18} =$ 12. $2\dfrac{2}{5} + 3\dfrac{3}{15} =$

Multiply the fractions and mixed numbers. Change to simplest form.

13. $\dfrac{5}{7} \times \dfrac{2}{7} =$ 14. $2 \times \dfrac{1}{3} =$ 15. $\dfrac{5}{8} \times \dfrac{3}{8} =$ 16. $\dfrac{1}{2} \times \dfrac{4}{5} =$

17. $4\dfrac{1}{4} \times 2\dfrac{3}{4} =$ 18. $2\dfrac{7}{8} \times 6\dfrac{2}{3} =$ 19. $2\dfrac{3}{5} \times 5\dfrac{1}{2} =$

Add or subtract.

20.   3.1   21.   5.9   22.   74.06   23.   86.29   24.   406.34
    + 6.2   + 4.2   – 3.1   +   .03   – 26.12

25. 42.5 + 1.8 =   26. 34.23 + 16.5 =

27. 13.1 + 5.5 =   28. 45.31 – 17.2 =

Total Problems _28_ Problems Correct_____

93

Multiply or divide.

1. **12**
    x 3.4

2. **23**
    x .16

3. **9.63**
    x 12.2

4. **.953**
    x   .7

5. **.75**
    x .3

6. $5\overline{)18.5}$

7. $.27\overline{)224.1}$

8. $8\overline{)25.6}$

9. $16\overline{)89.6}$

10. **12 x 1.2 = _____**

11. **2.84 x 16.5 = _____**

12. **89.6 ÷ 16 = _____**

13. **25.6 ÷ 8 = _____**

14. **.75 x 3 = _____**

15. **.3 x 75 = _____**

16. **.996 ÷ 12 = _____**

17. **30 ÷ .25 = _____**

18. **.721 ÷ 7 = _____**

19. **10 ÷ .20 = _____**

20. **.50 ÷ 2 = _____**

21. **70 ÷ .35 = _____**

Total Problems __21__ Problems Correct ____

Change each decimal to a fraction.

1. $5.2 =$ **2.** $.5 =$ **3.** $6.4 =$ **4.** $2.52 =$ **5.** $12.36 =$

Change each fraction or mixed number to a decimal.

6. $\dfrac{1}{8} =$ **7.** $\dfrac{3}{4} =$ **8.** $2\dfrac{3}{8} =$ **9.** $5\dfrac{3}{4} =$ **10.** $3\dfrac{3}{5} =$

Draw and label the following.

11. Line Segment ST

12. Line PQ

13. Angle XYZ

14. Pentagon EFGHI

15. Circle G, with Radius GH

Fill in the blank with the correct equivalent.

16. 1 yard =_____ feet

17. 1 foot =_____ inches

18. 1 mile =_____ yards

19. 1 yard =_____ inches

20. 1 meter =_____ centimeters

21. 1 centimeter =_____ meters

22. 1 meter =_____ kilometers

Total Problems __22__ Problems Correct _____

Answer Key

Name_____ Skill: Adding One and Two Digit Numbers

Page 1 — Skill: Adding One and Two Digit Numbers

Add.

1. 53 + 6 = 59	2. 42 + 7 = 49	3. 25 + 3 = 28	4. 36 + 2 = 38	5. 41 + 7 = 48
6. 25 + 5 = 30	7. 17 + 9 = 26	8. 10 + 2 = 12	9. 49 + 8 = 57	10. 65 + 9 = 74
11. 72 + 6 = 78	12. 85 + 4 = 89	13. 97 + 2 = 99	14. 65 + 1 = 66	15. 39 + 4 = 43
16. 22 + 6 = 28	17. 45 + 3 = 48	18. 69 + 8 = 77	19. 72 + 4 = 76	20. 87 + 9 = 96
21. 56 + 4 = 60	22. 65 + 8 = 73	23. 17 + 7 = 24	24. 26 + 7 = 33	25. 30 + 8 = 38
26. 14 + 9 = 23	27. 38 + 6 = 44	28. 51 + 7 = 58	29. 62 + 4 = 66	30. 43 + 5 = 48

Total Problems 30   Problems Correct ____

© Carson-Dellosa CD-3747   1

Page 2 — Skill: Adding Two Digit Numbers

Add.

1. 36 + 54 = 90	2. 42 + 17 = 59	3. 85 + 12 = 97	4. 99 + 1 = 100	5. 25 + 15 = 40
6. 53 + 53 = 106	7. 22 + 16 = 38	8. 36 + 33 = 69	9. 79 + 16 = 95	10. 42 + 18 = 60
11. 12 + 24 = 36	12. 60 + 32 = 92	13. 48 + 72 = 120	14. 63 + 49 = 112	15. 89 + 11 = 100
16. 51 + 19 = 70	17. 40 + 30 = 70	18. 92 + 86 = 178	19. 83 + 25 = 108	20. 47 + 39 = 86
21. 28 + 27 = 55	22. 53 + 10 = 63	23. 43 + 21 = 64	24. 78 + 65 = 143	25. 90 + 62 = 152
26. 91 + 33 = 124	27. 25 + 25 = 50	28. 57 + 31 = 88	29. 87 + 14 = 101	30. 92 + 27 = 119

Total Problems 30   Problems Correct ____

© Carson-Dellosa CD-3747   2

Page 3 — Skill: Adding Three and Four Digit Numbers

Add.

1. 4,237 + 201 = 4,438	2. 5,968 + 525 = 6,493	3. 6,010 + 902 = 6,912	4. 7,546 + 323 = 7,869	5. 4,870 + 106 = 4,976
6. 9,841 + 520 = 10,361	7. 8,211 + 345 = 8,556	8. 9,076 + 153 = 9,229	9. 1,120 + 782 = 1,902	10. 2,436 + 618 = 3,054
11. 3,011 + 654 = 3,665	12. 8,432 + 137 = 8,569	13. 6,509 + 225 = 6,734	14. 6,029 + 367 = 6,396	15. 5,843 + 492 = 6,335
16. 4,472 + 689 = 5,161	17. 5,072 + 549 = 5,621	18. 2,389 + 422 = 2,811	19. 1,760 + 195 = 1,955	20. 7,352 + 254 = 7,606
21. 4,870 + 287 = 5,157	22. 6,580 + 871 = 7,451	23. 3,653 + 321 = 3,974	24. 4,661 + 128 = 4,789	25. 2,704 + 202 = 2,906

Total Problems 25   Problems Correct ____

© Carson-Dellosa CD-3747   3

Page 4 — Skill: Adding Three and Four Digit Numbers

Add.

1. 7,456 + 214 = 7,670	2. 5,057 + 421 = 5,478	3. 4,555 + 701 = 5,256	4. 9,879 + 256 = 10,135	5. 2,124 + 578 = 2,702
6. 4,888 + 247 = 5,135	7. 6,244 + 652 = 6,896	8. 8,247 + 920 = 9,167	9. 3,121 + 322 = 3,443	10. 2,259 + 621 = 2,880
11. 5,016 + 214 = 5,230	12. 8,885 + 546 = 9,431	13. 1,657 + 111 = 1,768	14. 2,456 + 108 = 2,564	15. 5,241 + 568 = 5,809
16. 4,111 + 287 = 4,398	17. 2,255 + 303 = 2,558	18. 3,147 + 434 = 3,581	19. 1,852 + 369 = 2,221	20. 7,745 + 325 = 8,070
21. 4,495 + 712 = 5,207	22. 7,843 + 367 = 8,210	23. 2,829 + 197 = 3,026	24. 3,715 + 246 = 3,961	25. 2,951 + 314 = 3,265

Total Problems 25   Problems Correct ____

© Carson-Dellosa CD-3747   4

Answer Key

Name_____   Skill: Adding Three and Four Digit Numbers

Add.

1. 1,526 + 718 **2,244**	2. 4,159 + 936 **5,095**	3. 4,963 + 173 **5,136**	4. 6,879 + 316 **7,195**	5. 1,258 + 648 **1,906**
6. 3,804 + 207 **4,011**	7. 6,943 + 309 **7,252**	8. 2,488 + 395 **2,883**	9. 3,977 + 478 **4,455**	10. 2,655 + 165 **2,820**
11. 4,358 + 885 **5,243**	12. 6,200 + 356 **6,556**	13. 4,650 + 121 **4,771**	14. 2,456 + 522 **2,978**	15. 5,651 + 786 **6,437**
16. 5,145 + 788 **5,933**	17. 2,960 + 785 **3,745**	18. 4,540 + 124 **4,664**	19. 1,865 + 750 **2,615**	20. 6,441 + 220 **6,661**
21. 7,321 + 992 **8,313**	22. 2,635 + 223 **2,858**	23. 2,564 + 852 **3,416**	24. 3,245 + 321 **3,566**	25. 3,251 + 775 **4,026**

Total Problems _25_ Problems Correct ____

5

Name_____   Skill: Adding Three Digit Numbers

Add.

1. 453 125 + 678 **1,256**	2. 987 642 + 325 **1,954**	3. 202 169 + 584 **955**	4. 376 825 + 916 **2,117**	5. 500 627 + 220 **1,347**
6. 143 225 + 336 **704**	7. 942 787 + 527 **2,256**	8. 609 333 + 175 **1,117**	9. 210 422 + 871 **1,503**	10. 904 409 + 105 **1,418**
11. 612 717 + 246 **1,575**	12. 240 135 + 167 **542**	13. 892 357 + 418 **1,667**	14. 275 245 + 106 **626**	15. 318 771 + 522 **1,611**
16. 818 529 332 + 106 **1,785**	17. 954 623 873 + 480 **2,930**	18. 987 789 102 + 201 **2,079**	19. 123 497 675 + 542 **1,837**	20. 901 801 710 + 410 **2,822**
21. 533 397 864 + 702 **2,496**	22. 405 612 935 + 360 **2,312**	23. 220 115 780 + 650 **1,765**	24. 771 860 550 + 137 **2,318**	25. 147 257 662 + 770 **1,836**

Total Problems _25_ Problems Correct ____

6

Name_____   Skill: Adding One, Two, Three, and Four Digit Numbers

Add.

1. 2,671
   52
  125
+ 406
3,254
	2. 35
	 403
	3,850
	+ 16
	4,304
		3. 17
		 62
		 54
		+ 2,560
		2,693
			4. 8,430
			 217
			  32
			+ 2,560
			11,239
				5. 97
				621
				503
				+ 7
				1,228

6. 7,732
 806
  54
+ 325
8,917
	7. 6,210
	5,332
	  15
	+ 407
	11,964
		8. 3,275
		3,902
		7,340
		+ 803
		15,320
			9. 3,243
			8,395
			  43
			+ 731
			12,412
				10. 6,035
				  63
				532
				+ 172
				6,802

11. 5,306
  92
  24
+ 525
5,947
	12. 2,591
	2,624
	  33
	+ 106
	5,354
		13. 4,305
		307
		 34
		+ 67
		4,713
			14. 9,876
			1,445
			 324
			+ 225
			11,870
				15. 3,298
				867
				 54
				+ 144
				4,363

16. 8,214
 248
  17
+ 200
8,679
	17. 9,200
	   3
	 146
	+ 408
	9,757
		18. 3,084
		  26
		 192
		+ 764
		4,066
			19. 21
			403
			809
			+ 4,321
			5,554
				20. 726
				 50
				  4
				+ 9,210
				9,990

Total Problems _20_ Problems Correct ____

7

Name_____   Skill: Subtracting One and Two Digit Numbers

Subtract.

1. 35 − 5 **30**	2. 42 − 7 **35**	3. 18 − 9 **9**	4. 27 − 3 **24**	5. 59 − 8 **51**
6. 62 − 9 **53**	7. 47 − 8 **39**	8. 25 − 3 **22**	9. 33 − 5 **28**	10. 49 − 6 **43**
11. 51 − 7 **44**	12. 62 − 5 **57**	13. 84 − 5 **79**	14. 92 − 9 **83**	15. 76 − 7 **69**
16. 64 − 3 **61**	17. 87 − 5 **82**	18. 97 − 4 **93**	19. 92 − 10 **82**	20. 32 − 6 **26**
21. 25 − 14 **11**	22. 88 − 27 **61**	23. 95 − 64 **31**	24. 75 − 43 **32**	25. 53 − 2 **51**
26. 73 − 62 **11**	27. 86 − 29 **57**	28. 32 − 28 **4**	29. 56 − 26 **30**	30. 28 − 3 **25**

Total Problems _30_ Problems Correct ____

8

Answer Key

Name_____

Skill: Subtracting Two, Three, and Four Digit Numbers

Subtract.

1.	2.	3.	4.	5.
302 − 25 **227**	604 − 52 **552**	479 − 63 **416**	527 − 49 **478**	275 − 25 **250**

6.	7.	8.	9.	10.
800 − 72 **728**	133 − 54 **79**	175 − 87 **88**	992 − 36 **956**	689 − 56 **633**

11.	12.	13.	14.	15.
154 − 109 **45**	387 − 275 **112**	488 − 243 **245**	767 − 516 **251**	879 − 437 **442**

16.	17.	18.	19.	20.
2,487 − 333 **2,154**	5,879 − 631 **5,248**	1,250 − 758 **492**	6,840 − 522 **6,318**	3,807 − 416 **3,391**

21.	22.	23.	24.	25.
4,176 − 328 **3,848**	5,912 − 756 **5,156**	7,895 − 167 **7,728**	1,786 − 250 **1,536**	4,834 − 956 **3,878**

Total Problems _25_ Problems Correct ____

9

Name_____

Skill: Subtracting Four and Five Digit Numbers

Subtract.

1.	2.	3.	4.
30,821 − 4,163 **26,658**	52,964 − 3,175 **49,789**	87,576 − 6,353 **81,223**	83,542 − 6,427 **77,115**

5.	6.	7.	8.
72,541 − 8,530 **64,011**	76,283 − 7,657 **68,626**	94,443 − 7,785 **86,658**	62,083 − 7,228 **54,855**

9.	10.	11.	12.
44,785 − 27,556 **17,229**	35,463 − 27,540 **7,923**	46,724 − 20,407 **26,317**	72,450 − 36,000 **36,450**

13.	14.	15.	16.
42,165 − 30,708 **11,457**	40,081 − 21,721 **18,360**	31,621 − 23,126 **8,495**	92,140 − 12,306 **79,834**

Total Problems _16_ Problems Correct ____

10

Name_____

Skill: Multiplying One and Two Digit Numbers

Multiply.

1.	2.	3.	4.	5.
2 x 8 **16**	4 x 6 **24**	10 x 9 **90**	6 x 7 **42**	11 x 5 **55**

6.	7.	8.	9.	10.
8 x 8 **64**	3 x 7 **21**	4 x 8 **32**	9 x 5 **45**	3 x 9 **27**

11.	12.	13.	14.	15.
10 x 10 **100**	11 x 11 **121**	4 x 9 **36**	3 x 12 **36**	11 x 8 **88**

16.	17.	18.	19.	20.
7 x 7 **49**	6 x 6 **36**	5 x 5 **25**	3 x 4 **12**	10 x 2 **20**

21.	22.	23.	24.	25.
3 x 5 **15**	2 x 12 **24**	1 x 11 **11**	4 x 7 **28**	5 x 2 **10**

26.	27.	28.	29.	30.
12 x 4 **48**	6 x 9 **54**	15 x 2 **30**	13 x 3 **39**	18 x 1 **18**

Total Problems _30_ Problems Correct ____

11

Name_____

Skill: Multiplying One and Two Digit Numbers

Multiply.

1.	2.	3.	4.	5.
12 x 12 **144**	4 x 12 **48**	3 x 6 **18**	9 x 6 **54**	11 x 7 **77**

6.	7.	8.	9.	10.
9 x 9 **81**	4 x 10 **40**	9 x 11 **99**	7 x 12 **84**	11 x 12 **132**

11.	12.	13.	14.	15.
2 x 9 **18**	3 x 10 **30**	8 x 9 **72**	6 x 10 **60**	10 x 11 **110**

16.	17.	18.	19.	20.
4 x 7 **28**	5 x 12 **60**	2 x 11 **22**	6 x 12 **72**	6 x 8 **48**

21.	22.	23.	24.	25.
3 x 11 **33**	4 x 5 **20**	12 x 11 **132**	12 x 10 **120**	5 x 10 **50**

26.	27.	28.	29.	30.
3 x 8 **24**	4 x 4 **16**	6 x 9 **54**	9 x 9 **81**	12 x 3 **36**

Total Problems _30_ Problems Correct ____

12

Answer Key

Worksheet 13

Name_____

Skill: Multiplying One and Two Digit Numbers

Multiply.

1.	2.	3.	4.	5.
10 x 11 110	5 x 13 65	4 x 5 20	8 x 2 16	10 x 5 50

6.	7.	8.	9.	10.
7 x 10 70	5 x 11 55	6 x 10 60	4 x 10 40	17 x 12 204

11.	12.	13.	14.	15.
1 x 9 9	3 x 8 24	5 x 9 45	7 x 10 70	8 x 11 88

16.	17.	18.	19.	20.
3 x 7 21	4 x 11 44	3 x 10 30	1 x 12 12	2 x 8 16

21.	22.	23.	24.	25.
4 x 15 60	3 x 14 42	8 x 11 88	6 x 10 60	5 x 12 60

26.	27.	28.	29.	30.
1 x 8 8	2 x 4 8	3 x 9 27	9 x 8 72	1 x 4 4

Total Problems _30_ Problems Correct ____

© Carson-Dellosa CD-3747   13

Worksheet 14

Name_____

Skill: Multiplying One and Two Digit Numbers

Multiply.

1.	2.	3.	4.	5.
50 x 5 250	71 x 4 284	52 x 3 156	86 x 1 86	40 x 6 240

6.	7.	8.	9.	10.
21 x 3 63	82 x 4 328	33 x 3 99	12 x 4 48	22 x 3 66

11.	12.	13.	14.	15.
21 x 4 84	12 x 3 36	24 x 2 48	41 x 8 328	81 x 7 567

16.	17.	18.	19.	20.
51 x 4 204	11 x 3 33	71 x 6 426	91 x 5 455	92 x 0 0

21.	22.	23.	24.	25.
62 x 3 186	23 x 3 69	44 x 2 88	82 x 3 246	34 x 2 68

26.	27.	28.	29.	30.
24 x 2 48	22 x 4 88	14 x 2 28	52 x 4 208	63 x 3 189

Total Problems _30_ Problems Correct ____

© Carson-Dellosa CD-3747   14

Worksheet 15

Name_____

Skill: Multiplying One and Two Digit Numbers

Multiply.

1.	2.	3.	4.	5.
48 x 9 432	27 x 4 108	85 x 3 255	72 x 8 576	35 x 6 210

6.	7.	8.	9.	10.
28 x 3 84	56 x 2 112	82 x 7 574	69 x 3 207	34 x 3 102

11.	12.	13.	14.	15.
54 x 8 432	37 x 5 185	16 x 4 64	26 x 5 130	39 x 7 273

16.	17.	18.	19.	20.
82 x 6 492	77 x 7 539	53 x 8 424	62 x 5 310	43 x 6 258

21.	22.	23.	24.	25.
12 x 7 84	57 x 4 228	14 x 9 126	43 x 4 172	25 x 2 50

26.	27.	28.	29.	30.
53 x 5 265	34 x 9 306	46 x 5 230	78 x 6 468	25 x 7 175

Total Problems _30_ Problems Correct ____

© Carson-Dellosa CD-3747   15

Worksheet 16

Name_____

Skill: Multiplying One and Three Digit Numbers

Multiply.

1.	2.	3.	4.	5.
323 x 5 1,615	109 x 4 436	206 x 5 1,030	423 x 6 2,538	816 x 2 1,632

6.	7.	8.	9.	10.
515 x 4 2,060	812 x 8 6,496	617 x 7 4,319	415 x 2 830	815 x 7 5,705

11.	12.	13.	14.	15.
255 x 4 1,020	503 x 3 1,509	134 x 6 804	584 x 3 1,752	804 x 6 4,824

16.	17.	18.	19.	20.
915 x 2 1,830	827 x 3 2,481	905 x 5 4,525	234 x 5 1,170	316 x 7 2,212

21.	22.	23.	24.	25.
860 x 2 1,720	122 x 8 976	706 x 4 2,824	342 x 5 1,710	715 x 4 2,860

26.	27.	28.	29.	30.
861 x 9 7,749	523 x 6 3,138	422 x 5 2,110	256 x 5 1,280	121 x 9 1,089

Total Problems _30_ Problems Correct ____

© Carson-Dellosa CD-3747   16

Answer Key

Skill: Multiplying One and
Four Digit Numbers

Multiply.

1. 2,582 x 7 **18,074**	2. 4,108 x 2 **8,216**	3. 5,306 x 3 **15,918**	4. 1,029 x 5 **5,145**	5. 5,678 x 2 **11,356**
6. 3,232 x 4 **12,928**	7. 7,109 x 8 **56,872**	8. 6,241 x 7 **43,687**	9. 5,414 x 2 **10,828**	10. 4,610 x 5 **23,050**
11. 1,067 x 3 **3,201**	12. 2,000 x 6 **12,000**	13. 6,384 x 9 **57,456**	14. 6,501 x 7 **45,507**	15. 5,129 x 5 **25,645**
16. 3,610 x 4 **14,440**	17. 2,168 x 6 **13,008**	18. 4,634 x 2 **9,268**	19. 2,897 x 4 **11,588**	20. 3,162 x 4 **12,648**
21. 7,564 x 5 **37,820**	22. 6,528 x 9 **58,752**	23. 8,436 x 5 **42,180**	24. 7,152 x 4 **28,608**	25. 7,109 x 6 **42,654**
26. 5,831 x 4 **23,324**	27. 5,672 x 3 **17,016**	28. 5,691 x 5 **28,455**	29. 4,646 x 9 **41,814**	30. 4,862 x 7 **34,034**

Total Problems _30_ Problems Correct ____

17

Skill: Multiplying Two Digit Numbers

Multiply.

1. 41 x 18 **738**	2. 38 x 22 **836**	3. 64 x 47 **3,008**	4. 68 x 32 **2,176**	5. 72 x 43 **3,096**
6. 53 x 38 **2,014**	7. 36 x 12 **432**	8. 82 x 51 **4,182**	9. 42 x 18 **756**	10. 72 x 63 **4,536**
11. 53 x 46 **2,438**	12. 62 x 43 **2,666**	13. 25 x 17 **425**	14. 86 x 42 **3,612**	15. 83 x 27 **2,241**
16. 52 x 30 **1,560**	17. 81 x 72 **5,832**	18. 91 x 43 **3,913**	19. 35 x 28 **980**	20. 70 x 60 **4,200**
21. 86 x 75 **6,450**	22. 56 x 13 **728**	23. 49 x 28 **1,372**	24. 73 x 56 **4,088**	25. 54 x 27 **1,458**

Total Problems _25_ Problems Correct ____

18

Skill: Multiplying Two and
Three Digit Numbers

Multiply.

1. 518 x 42 **21,756**	2. 729 x 56 **40,824**	3. 455 x 31 **14,105**	4. 512 x 60 **30,720**	5. 485 x 21 **10,185**
6. 216 x 10 **2,160**	7. 591 x 19 **11,229**	8. 327 x 35 **11,445**	9. 244 x 32 **7,808**	10. 123 x 46 **5,658**
11. 443 x 33 **14,619**	12. 248 x 75 **18,600**	13. 697 x 46 **32,062**	14. 843 x 12 **10,116**	15. 695 x 61 **42,395**
16. 687 x 51 **35,037**	17. 792 x 43 **34,056**	18. 826 x 26 **21,476**	19. 746 x 37 **27,602**	20. 792 x 49 **38,808**
21. 554 x 53 **29,362**	22. 456 x 14 **6,384**	23. 647 x 18 **11,646**	24. 535 x 79 **42,265**	25. 691 x 24 **16,584**

Total Problems _25_ Problems Correct ____

19

Skill: Multiplying Three Digit Numbers

Multiply.

1. 654 x 132 **86,328**	2. 221 x 103 **22,763**	3. 416 x 122 **50,752**	4. 412 x 203 **83,636**	5. 321 x 324 **104,004**
6. 542 x 172 **93,224**	7. 365 x 184 **67,160**	8. 593 x 347 **205,771**	9. 827 x 579 **478,833**	10. 427 x 273 **116,571**
11. 323 x 247 **79,781**	12. 756 x 633 **478,548**	13. 724 x 377 **272,948**	14. 520 x 397 **206,440**	15. 678 x 459 **311,202**
16. 826 x 825 **681,450**	17. 236 x 420 **99,120**	18. 351 x 240 **84,240**	19. 630 x 141 **88,830**	20. 517 x 510 **263,670**
21. 340 x 285 **96,900**	22. 630 x 246 **154,980**	23. 577 x 290 **167,330**	24. 770 x 143 **110,110**	25. 370 x 237 **87,690**

Total Problems _25_ Problems Correct ____

20

Answer Key

Page 21

Name_____ Skill: Dividing by One Digit Numbers
—No Remainders

Divide.

1. $3\overline{\smash{)}12}$ = 4
2. $4\overline{\smash{)}24}$ = 6
3. $5\overline{\smash{)}10}$ = 2
4. $3\overline{\smash{)}9}$ = 3
5. $2\overline{\smash{)}8}$ = 4

6. $4\overline{\smash{)}12}$ = 3
7. $5\overline{\smash{)}15}$ = 3
8. $6\overline{\smash{)}42}$ = 7
9. $6\overline{\smash{)}54}$ = 9
10. $7\overline{\smash{)}63}$ = 9

11. $8\overline{\smash{)}48}$ = 6
12. $9\overline{\smash{)}72}$ = 8
13. $7\overline{\smash{)}42}$ = 6
14. $4\overline{\smash{)}28}$ = 7
15. $8\overline{\smash{)}56}$ = 7

16. $30 \div 5 = \underline{6}$
17. $12 \div 6 = \underline{2}$
18. $36 \div 9 = \underline{4}$

19. $35 \div 7 = \underline{5}$
20. $21 \div 7 = \underline{3}$
21. $32 \div 4 = \underline{8}$

22. $14 \div 7 = \underline{2}$
23. $24 \div 6 = \underline{4}$
24. $20 \div 5 = \underline{4}$

25. $36 \div 9 = \underline{4}$
26. $64 \div 8 = \underline{8}$
27. $18 \div 6 = \underline{3}$

Total Problems _27_ Problems Correct ____

21

Page 22

Name_____ Skill: Dividing by One Digit Numbers
—No Remainders

Divide.

1. $6\overline{\smash{)}72}$ = 12
2. $7\overline{\smash{)}98}$ = 14
3. $3\overline{\smash{)}36}$ = 12
4. $2\overline{\smash{)}24}$ = 12
5. $8\overline{\smash{)}80}$ = 10

6. $5\overline{\smash{)}90}$ = 18
7. $4\overline{\smash{)}72}$ = 18
8. $7\overline{\smash{)}70}$ = 10
9. $6\overline{\smash{)}84}$ = 14
10. $2\overline{\smash{)}86}$ = 43

11. $3\overline{\smash{)}93}$ = 31
12. $7\overline{\smash{)}91}$ = 13
13. $8\overline{\smash{)}88}$ = 11
14. $9\overline{\smash{)}99}$ = 11
15. $4\overline{\smash{)}96}$ = 24

16. $2\overline{\smash{)}36}$ = 18
17. $4\overline{\smash{)}40}$ = 10
18. $5\overline{\smash{)}55}$ = 11
19. $9\overline{\smash{)}90}$ = 10
20. $3\overline{\smash{)}45}$ = 15

21. $3\overline{\smash{)}96}$ = 32
22. $7\overline{\smash{)}84}$ = 12
23. $5\overline{\smash{)}55}$ = 11
24. $3\overline{\smash{)}75}$ = 25
25. $5\overline{\smash{)}85}$ = 17

26. $3\overline{\smash{)}66}$ = 22
27. $6\overline{\smash{)}78}$ = 13
28. $5\overline{\smash{)}90}$ = 18
29. $3\overline{\smash{)}51}$ = 17
30. $8\overline{\smash{)}96}$ = 12

Total Problems _30_ Problems Correct ____

22

Page 23

Name_____ Skill: Dividing by One Digit Numbers
—No Remainders

Divide.

1. $9\overline{\smash{)}1,368}$ = 152
2. $7\overline{\smash{)}2,926}$ = 418
3. $6\overline{\smash{)}2,706}$ = 451
4. $5\overline{\smash{)}1,125}$ = 225

5. $4\overline{\smash{)}1,228}$ = 307
6. $4\overline{\smash{)}1,008}$ = 252
7. $3\overline{\smash{)}2,019}$ = 673
8. $2\overline{\smash{)}1,024}$ = 512

9. $8\overline{\smash{)}5,392}$ = 674
10. $5\overline{\smash{)}975}$ = 195
11. $3\overline{\smash{)}1,008}$ = 336
12. $9\overline{\smash{)}1,134}$ = 126

13. $6\overline{\smash{)}1,878}$ = 313
14. $4\overline{\smash{)}2,128}$ = 532
15. $8\overline{\smash{)}3,888}$ = 486
16. $8\overline{\smash{)}4,960}$ = 620

17. $5\overline{\smash{)}1,395}$ = 279
18. $2\overline{\smash{)}1,224}$ = 612
19. $7\overline{\smash{)}1,421}$ = 203
20. $9\overline{\smash{)}2,790}$ = 310

Total Problems _20_ Problems Correct ____

23

Page 24

Name_____ Skill: Dividing by One Digit Numbers
—with Remainders

Divide.

1. $7\overline{\smash{)}82}$ = 11 r5
2. $8\overline{\smash{)}95}$ = 11 r7
3. $4\overline{\smash{)}63}$ = 15 r3
4. $5\overline{\smash{)}81}$ = 15 r6
5. $6\overline{\smash{)}74}$ = 12 r2

6. $4\overline{\smash{)}54}$ = 13 r2
7. $4\overline{\smash{)}18}$ = 4 r2
8. $5\overline{\smash{)}22}$ = 4 r2
9. $4\overline{\smash{)}41}$ = 10 r1
10. $8\overline{\smash{)}37}$ = 4 r5

11. $3\overline{\smash{)}26}$ = 8 r2
12. $7\overline{\smash{)}57}$ = 8 r1
13. $5\overline{\smash{)}18}$ = 3 r3
14. $3\overline{\smash{)}29}$ = 9 r2
15. $5\overline{\smash{)}42}$ = 8 r2

16. $23 \div 5 = \underline{4\ r3}$
17. $45 \div 6 = \underline{7\ r3}$
18. $25 \div 3 = \underline{8\ r1}$

19. $58 \div 7 = \underline{8\ r2}$
20. $51 \div 7 = \underline{7\ r2}$
21. $43 \div 2 = \underline{21\ r1}$

22. $46 \div 5 = \underline{9\ r1}$
23. $32 \div 6 = \underline{5\ r2}$
24. $19 \div 2 = \underline{9\ r1}$

25. $24 \div 7 = \underline{3\ r3}$
26. $26 \div 3 = \underline{8\ r2}$
27. $87 \div 9 = \underline{9\ r6}$

Total Problems _27_ Problems Correct ____

24

Answer Key

Worksheet (page 25)

Name_____   Skill: Dividing by One Digit Numbers
—with Remainders

Divide.

1. $6\overline{)82} = 13\ r4$
2. $3\overline{)59} = 19\ r2$
3. $4\overline{)97} = 24\ r1$
4. $5\overline{)63} = 12\ r3$
5. $3\overline{)67} = 22\ r1$

6. $2\overline{)39} = 19\ r1$
7. $6\overline{)82} = 13\ r4$
8. $8\overline{)97} = 12\ r1$
9. $5\overline{)83} = 16\ r3$
10. $5\overline{)63} = 12\ r3$

11. $8\overline{)89} = 11\ r1$
12. $2\overline{)81} = 40\ r1$
13. $7\overline{)92} = 13\ r1$
14. $7\overline{)81} = 11\ r4$
15. $6\overline{)73} = 12\ r1$

16. $4\overline{)85} = 21\ r1$
17. $2\overline{)23} = 11\ r1$
18. $7\overline{)93} = 13\ r2$
19. $6\overline{)85} = 14\ r1$
20. $3\overline{)83} = 27\ r2$

21. $4\overline{)70} = 17\ r2$
22. $8\overline{)94} = 11\ r6$
23. $7\overline{)79} = 11\ r2$
24. $6\overline{)89} = 14\ r5$
25. $7\overline{)85} = 12\ r1$

26. $7\overline{)93} = 13\ r2$
27. $5\overline{)82} = 16\ r2$
28. $6\overline{)89} = 14\ r5$
29. $9\overline{)98} = 10\ r8$
30. $3\overline{)47} = 15\ r2$

Total Problems 30 Problems Correct ____

25

Worksheet (page 26)

Name_____   Skill: Dividing by One Digit Numbers
—with Remainders

Divide.

1. $4\overline{)873} = 218\ r1$
2. $5\overline{)527} = 105\ r2$
3. $3\overline{)784} = 261\ r1$
4. $4\overline{)862} = 215\ r2$

5. $5\overline{)943} = 188\ r3$
6. $2\overline{)597} = 298\ r1$
7. $4\overline{)486} = 121\ r2$
8. $2\overline{)733} = 366\ r1$

9. $8\overline{)957} = 119\ r5$
10. $9\overline{)973} = 108\ r1$
11. $3\overline{)629} = 209\ r2$
12. $8\overline{)937} = 117\ r1$

13. $9\overline{)987} = 109\ r6$
14. $4\overline{)574} = 143\ r2$
15. $2\overline{)301} = 150\ r1$
16. $3\overline{)574} = 191\ r1$

17. $7\overline{)915} = 130\ r5$
18. $6\overline{)653} = 108\ r5$
19. $5\overline{)637} = 127\ r2$
20. $4\overline{)653} = 163\ r1$

Total Problems 20 Problems Correct ____

26

Worksheet (page 27)

Name_____   Skill: Dividing by Two Digit Numbers
—No Remainders

Divide.

1. $32\overline{)512} = 16$
2. $41\overline{)820} = 20$
3. $15\overline{)540} = 36$
4. $26\overline{)338} = 13$

5. $52\overline{)624} = 12$
6. $12\overline{)144} = 12$
7. $73\overline{)365} = 5$
8. $25\overline{)350} = 14$

9. $18\overline{)450} = 25$
10. $32\overline{)960} = 30$
11. $56\overline{)952} = 17$
12. $45\overline{)990} = 22$

13. $32\overline{)768} = 24$
14. $18\overline{)702} = 39$
15. $47\overline{)517} = 11$
16. $24\overline{)600} = 25$

17. $62\overline{)992} = 16$
18. $39\overline{)858} = 22$
19. $27\overline{)810} = 30$
20. $54\overline{)864} = 16$

Total Problems 20 Problems Correct ____

27

Worksheet (page 28)

Name_____   Skill: Dividing by Two Digit Numbers
—with Remainders

Divide.

1. $67\overline{)807} = 12\ r3$
2. $58\overline{)368} = 6\ r20$
3. $25\overline{)465} = 18\ r15$
4. $45\overline{)787} = 17\ r22$

5. $37\overline{)369} = 9\ r36$
6. $18\overline{)652} = 36\ r4$
7. $11\overline{)505} = 45\ r10$
8. $22\overline{)268} = 12\ r4$

9. $64\overline{)654} = 10\ r14$
10. $23\overline{)875} = 38\ r1$
11. $19\overline{)410} = 21\ r11$
12. $42\overline{)632} = 15\ r2$

13. $81\overline{)921} = 11\ r30$
14. $13\overline{)235} = 18\ r1$
15. $32\overline{)458} = 14\ r10$
16. $56\overline{)647} = 11\ r31$

17. $61\overline{)741} = 12\ r9$
18. $40\overline{)142} = 3\ r22$
19. $53\overline{)367} = 6\ r49$
20. $87\overline{)357} = 4\ r9$

Total Problems 20 Problems Correct ____

28

102

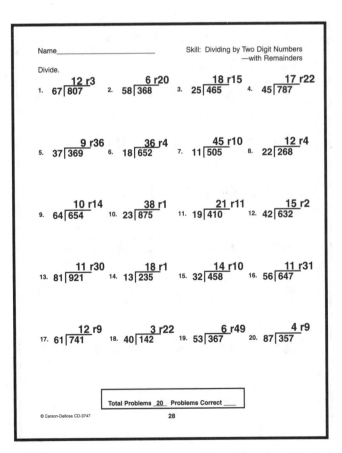

Answer Key

Name_____   Skill: Dividing by Two Digit Numbers
                                        —with Remainders

Divide.

1. $43\overline{)1,256}$ **29 r9**   2. $21\overline{)3,010}$ **143 r7**   3. $30\overline{)6,172}$ **205 r22**   4. $59\overline{)8,787}$ **148 r55**

5. $48\overline{)2,541}$ **52 r45**   6. $39\overline{)8,563}$ **219 r22**   7. $78\overline{)5,000}$ **64 r8**   8. $55\overline{)9,999}$ **181 r44**

9. $65\overline{)1,596}$ **24 r36**   10. $82\overline{)4,512}$ **55 r2**   11. $77\overline{)2,159}$ **28 r3**   12. $27\overline{)3,265}$ **120 r25**

13. $22\overline{)7,321}$ **332 r17**   14. $37\overline{)2,148}$ **58 r2**   15. $85\overline{)3,578}$ **42 r8**   16. $56\overline{)5,892}$ **105 r12**

Total Problems __16__ Problems Correct ____

29

Name_____   Skill: Learning about Fractions

Shade in the part of each shape that equals the given fraction.

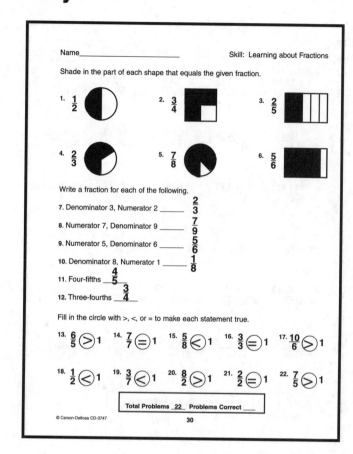

1. $\frac{1}{2}$ 2. $\frac{3}{4}$ 3. $\frac{2}{5}$

4. $\frac{2}{3}$ 5. $\frac{7}{8}$ 6. $\frac{5}{6}$

Write a fraction for each of the following.

7. Denominator 3, Numerator 2 _____ $\frac{2}{3}$

8. Numerator 7, Denominator 9 _____ $\frac{7}{9}$

9. Numerator 5, Denominator 6 _____ $\frac{5}{6}$

10. Denominator 8, Numerator 1 _____ $\frac{1}{8}$

11. Four-fifths _____ $\frac{4}{5}$

12. Three-fourths _____ $\frac{3}{4}$

Fill in the circle with >, <, or = to make each statement true.

13. $\frac{6}{5} \gtrdot 1$ 14. $\frac{7}{7} = 1$ 15. $\frac{5}{8} < 1$ 16. $\frac{3}{3} = 1$ 17. $\frac{10}{6} > 1$

18. $\frac{1}{2} < 1$ 19. $\frac{3}{7} < 1$ 20. $\frac{8}{2} > 1$ 21. $\frac{2}{2} = 1$ 22. $\frac{7}{5} > 1$

Total Problems __22__ Problems Correct ____

30

Name_____   Skill: Changing Fractions to Simplest Form

Change each fraction to simplest form.

1. $\frac{6}{8} = \frac{3}{4}$ 2. $\frac{5}{20} = \frac{1}{4}$ 3. $\frac{3}{12} = \frac{1}{4}$ 4. $\frac{2}{8} = \frac{1}{4}$ 5. $\frac{10}{12} = \frac{5}{6}$

6. $\frac{3}{24} = \frac{1}{8}$ 7. $\frac{4}{8} = \frac{1}{2}$ 8. $\frac{5}{15} = \frac{1}{3}$ 9. $\frac{14}{21} = \frac{2}{3}$ 10. $\frac{16}{24} = \frac{2}{3}$

11. $\frac{20}{35} = \frac{4}{7}$ 12. $\frac{4}{16} = \frac{1}{4}$ 13. $\frac{8}{16} = \frac{1}{2}$ 14. $\frac{12}{16} = \frac{3}{4}$ 15. $\frac{6}{18} = \frac{1}{3}$

16. $\frac{15}{20} = \frac{3}{4}$ 17. $\frac{6}{9} = \frac{2}{3}$ 18. $\frac{7}{21} = \frac{1}{3}$ 19. $\frac{16}{32} = \frac{1}{2}$ 20. $\frac{5}{10} = \frac{1}{2}$

21. $\frac{10}{20} = \frac{1}{2}$ 22. $\frac{4}{16} = \frac{1}{4}$ 23. $\frac{5}{25} = \frac{1}{5}$ 24. $\frac{7}{35} = \frac{1}{5}$ 25. $\frac{24}{32} = \frac{3}{4}$

26. $\frac{6}{16} = \frac{3}{8}$ 27. $\frac{3}{15} = \frac{1}{5}$ 28. $\frac{15}{30} = \frac{1}{2}$ 29. $\frac{17}{34} = \frac{1}{2}$ 30. $\frac{20}{40} = \frac{1}{2}$

Total Problems __30__ Problems Correct ____

31

Name_____   Skill: Changing Fractions to Simplest Form

Change each fraction to simplest form.

1. $\frac{4}{8} = \frac{1}{2}$ 2. $\frac{4}{12} = \frac{1}{3}$ 3. $\frac{3}{9} = \frac{1}{3}$ 4. $\frac{2}{4} = \frac{1}{2}$ 5. $\frac{12}{15} = \frac{4}{5}$

6. $\frac{7}{14} = \frac{1}{2}$ 7. $\frac{2}{8} = \frac{1}{4}$ 8. $\frac{8}{24} = \frac{1}{3}$ 9. $\frac{15}{21} = \frac{5}{7}$ 10. $\frac{18}{24} = \frac{3}{4}$

11. $\frac{20}{30} = \frac{2}{3}$ 12. $\frac{5}{30} = \frac{1}{6}$ 13. $\frac{8}{20} = \frac{2}{5}$ 14. $\frac{12}{30} = \frac{2}{5}$ 15. $\frac{4}{18} = \frac{2}{9}$

16. $\frac{10}{28} = \frac{5}{14}$ 17. $\frac{3}{9} = \frac{1}{3}$ 18. $\frac{6}{18} = \frac{1}{3}$ 19. $\frac{20}{22} = \frac{10}{11}$ 20. $\frac{5}{15} = \frac{1}{3}$

21. $\frac{14}{40} = \frac{7}{20}$ 22. $\frac{2}{6} = \frac{1}{3}$ 23. $\frac{5}{20} = \frac{1}{4}$ 24. $\frac{7}{28} = \frac{1}{4}$ 25. $\frac{15}{50} = \frac{3}{10}$

26. $\frac{6}{20} = \frac{3}{10}$ 27. $\frac{3}{15} = \frac{1}{5}$ 28. $\frac{15}{20} = \frac{3}{4}$ 29. $\frac{16}{32} = \frac{1}{2}$ 30. $\frac{21}{45} = \frac{7}{15}$

Total Problems __30__ Problems Correct ____

32

103

Answer Key

Name_____   Skill: Comparing Fractions

Fill in the circle with >, <, or = to make each statement true.

1. $\frac{16}{52}$ $<$ $\frac{16}{25}$ 2. $\frac{4}{5}$ $<$ $\frac{5}{6}$ 3. $\frac{7}{8}$ $>$ $\frac{5}{9}$

4. $\frac{13}{21}$ $<$ $\frac{10}{13}$ 5. $\frac{9}{10}$ $>$ $\frac{8}{15}$ 6. $\frac{1}{2}$ $>$ $\frac{24}{50}$

7. $\frac{16}{20}$ $>$ $\frac{10}{25}$ 8. $\frac{12}{24}$ $=$ $\frac{2}{4}$ 9. $\frac{18}{21}$ $>$ $\frac{12}{28}$

10. $\frac{12}{32}$ $<$ $\frac{12}{24}$ 11. $\frac{9}{15}$ $>$ $\frac{4}{10}$ 12. $\frac{9}{12}$ $=$ $\frac{15}{20}$

13. $\frac{14}{16}$ $>$ $\frac{15}{20}$ 14. $\frac{6}{15}$ $>$ $\frac{4}{20}$ 15. $\frac{35}{39}$ $>$ $\frac{14}{24}$

16. $\frac{56}{88}$ $>$ $\frac{25}{55}$ 17. $\frac{16}{36}$ $<$ $\frac{24}{27}$ 18. $\frac{16}{24}$ $=$ $\frac{20}{30}$

19. $\frac{16}{16}$ $=$ $\frac{25}{25}$ 20. $\frac{25}{30}$ $>$ $\frac{3}{18}$ 21. $\frac{21}{35}$ $<$ $\frac{16}{24}$

Total Problems _21_ Problems Correct ____

   33

Name_____   Skill: Changing Fractions to Mixed Numbers

Change each improper fraction to a mixed number.

1. $\frac{4}{3} = 1\frac{1}{3}$ 2. $\frac{5}{3} = 1\frac{2}{3}$ 3. $\frac{10}{4} = 2\frac{1}{2}$ 4. $\frac{6}{4} = 1\frac{1}{2}$ 5. $\frac{10}{3} = 3\frac{1}{3}$

6. $\frac{20}{15} = 1\frac{1}{3}$ 7. $\frac{12}{5} = 2\frac{2}{5}$ 8. $\frac{19}{2} = 9\frac{1}{2}$ 9. $\frac{43}{7} = 6\frac{1}{7}$ 10. $\frac{24}{10} = 2\frac{2}{5}$

11. $\frac{7}{4} = 1\frac{3}{4}$ 12. $\frac{13}{4} = 3\frac{1}{4}$ 13. $\frac{27}{5} = 5\frac{2}{5}$ 14. $\frac{19}{11} = 1\frac{8}{11}$ 15. $\frac{9}{8} = 1\frac{1}{8}$

16. $\frac{55}{12} = 4\frac{7}{12}$ 17. $\frac{13}{4} = 3\frac{1}{4}$ 18. $\frac{15}{4} = 3\frac{3}{4}$ 19. $\frac{20}{7} = 2\frac{6}{7}$ 20. $\frac{16}{3} = 5\frac{1}{3}$

21. $\frac{18}{5} = 3\frac{3}{5}$ 22. $\frac{13}{2} = 6\frac{1}{2}$ 23. $\frac{8}{3} = 2\frac{2}{3}$ 24. $\frac{9}{4} = 2\frac{1}{4}$ 25. $\frac{10}{3} = 3\frac{1}{3}$

26. $\frac{5}{2} = 2\frac{1}{2}$ 27. $\frac{17}{9} = 1\frac{8}{9}$ 28. $\frac{15}{8} = 1\frac{7}{8}$ 29. $\frac{17}{4} = 4\frac{1}{4}$ 30. $\frac{50}{6} = 8\frac{1}{3}$

Total Problems _30_ Problems Correct ____

   34

Name_____   Skill: Changing Fractions to Mixed Numbers

Change each improper fraction to a mixed number.

1. $\frac{6}{4} = 1\frac{1}{2}$ 2. $\frac{7}{4} = 1\frac{3}{4}$ 3. $\frac{11}{3} = 3\frac{2}{3}$ 4. $\frac{8}{3} = 2\frac{2}{3}$ 5. $\frac{12}{5} = 2\frac{2}{5}$

6. $\frac{21}{12} = 1\frac{3}{4}$ 7. $\frac{13}{3} = 4\frac{1}{3}$ 8. $\frac{17}{4} = 4\frac{1}{4}$ 9. $\frac{33}{6} = 5\frac{1}{2}$ 10. $\frac{18}{11} = 1\frac{7}{11}$

11. $\frac{9}{4} = 2\frac{1}{4}$ 12. $\frac{14}{8} = 1\frac{3}{4}$ 13. $\frac{19}{2} = 9\frac{1}{2}$ 14. $\frac{14}{8} = 1\frac{3}{4}$ 15. $\frac{9}{2} = 4\frac{1}{2}$

16. $\frac{25}{11} = 2\frac{3}{11}$ 17. $\frac{16}{5} = 3\frac{1}{5}$ 18. $\frac{25}{3} = 8\frac{1}{3}$ 19. $\frac{21}{8} = 2\frac{5}{8}$ 20. $\frac{15}{4} = 3\frac{3}{4}$

21. $\frac{19}{5} = 3\frac{4}{5}$ 22. $\frac{13}{3} = 4\frac{1}{3}$ 23. $\frac{8}{3} = 2\frac{2}{3}$ 24. $\frac{7}{4} = 1\frac{3}{4}$ 25. $\frac{10}{6} = 1\frac{2}{3}$

26. $\frac{3}{2} = 1\frac{1}{2}$ 27. $\frac{14}{8} = 1\frac{3}{4}$ 28. $\frac{11}{6} = 1\frac{5}{6}$ 29. $\frac{13}{3} = 4\frac{1}{3}$ 30. $\frac{10}{4} = 2\frac{1}{2}$

Total Problems _30_ Problems Correct ____

   35

Name_____   Skill: Changing Fractions to Mixed Numbers

Change each improper fraction to a mixed number.

1. $\frac{9}{2} = 4\frac{1}{2}$ 2. $\frac{12}{5} = 2\frac{2}{5}$ 3. $\frac{11}{2} = 5\frac{1}{2}$ 4. $\frac{16}{3} = 5\frac{1}{3}$ 5. $\frac{11}{5} = 2\frac{1}{5}$

6. $\frac{51}{10} = 5\frac{1}{10}$ 7. $\frac{13}{7} = 1\frac{6}{7}$ 8. $\frac{17}{6} = 2\frac{5}{6}$ 9. $\frac{12}{5} = 2\frac{2}{5}$ 10. $\frac{15}{14} = 1\frac{1}{14}$

11. $\frac{19}{5} = 3\frac{4}{5}$ 12. $\frac{16}{9} = 1\frac{7}{9}$ 13. $\frac{25}{8} = 3\frac{1}{8}$ 14. $\frac{3}{2} = 1\frac{1}{2}$ 15. $\frac{6}{5} = 1\frac{1}{5}$

16. $\frac{8}{7} = 1\frac{1}{7}$ 17. $\frac{10}{6} = 1\frac{2}{3}$ 18. $\frac{11}{10} = 1\frac{1}{10}$ 19. $\frac{61}{3} = 20\frac{1}{3}$ 20. $\frac{15}{14} = 1\frac{1}{14}$

21. $\frac{14}{13} = 1\frac{1}{13}$ 22. $\frac{17}{7} = 2\frac{3}{7}$ 23. $\frac{19}{18} = 1\frac{1}{18}$ 24. $\frac{13}{12} = 1\frac{1}{12}$ 25. $\frac{19}{11} = 1\frac{8}{11}$

26. $\frac{8}{5} = 1\frac{3}{5}$ 27. $\frac{13}{11} = 1\frac{2}{11}$ 28. $\frac{26}{22} = 1\frac{2}{11}$ 29. $\frac{47}{13} = 3\frac{8}{13}$ 30. $\frac{10}{9} = 1\frac{1}{9}$

Total Problems _30_ Problems Correct ____

   36

Answer Key

Worksheet 37

Name_____ Skill: Changing Fractions to Mixed Numbers

Change each improper fraction to a mixed number or whole number.

1. $\frac{23}{15} = 1\frac{8}{15}$ 2. $\frac{32}{15} = 2\frac{2}{15}$ 3. $\frac{48}{5} = 9\frac{3}{5}$ 4. $\frac{26}{4} = 6\frac{1}{2}$ 5. $\frac{29}{7} = 4\frac{1}{7}$

6. $\frac{40}{24} = 1\frac{2}{3}$ 7. $\frac{89}{17} = 5\frac{4}{17}$ 8. $\frac{66}{50} = 1\frac{3}{25}$ 9. $\frac{44}{13} = 3\frac{5}{13}$ 10. $\frac{62}{9} = 6\frac{8}{9}$

11. $\frac{97}{33} = 2\frac{31}{33}$ 12. $\frac{26}{15} = 1\frac{11}{15}$ 13. $\frac{13}{3} = 4\frac{1}{3}$ 14. $\frac{24}{20} = 1\frac{1}{5}$ 15. $\frac{8}{3} = 2\frac{2}{3}$

16. $\frac{55}{12} = 4\frac{7}{12}$ 17. $\frac{13}{4} = 3\frac{1}{4}$ 18. $\frac{15}{3} = 5$ 19. $\frac{20}{7} = 2\frac{6}{7}$ 20. $\frac{16}{3} = 5\frac{1}{3}$

21. $\frac{26}{12} = 2\frac{1}{6}$ 22. $\frac{59}{25} = 2\frac{9}{25}$ 23. $\frac{6}{4} = 1\frac{1}{2}$ 24. $\frac{17}{6} = 2\frac{5}{6}$ 25. $\frac{20}{8} = 2\frac{1}{2}$

26. $\frac{36}{34} = 1\frac{1}{17}$ 27. $\frac{10}{8} = 1\frac{1}{4}$ 28. $\frac{64}{49} = 1\frac{15}{49}$ 29. $\frac{56}{11} = 5\frac{1}{11}$ 30. $\frac{35}{12} = 2\frac{11}{12}$

Total Problems 30 Problems Correct ____

Worksheet 38

Name_____ Skill: Changing Mixed Numbers to Improper Fractions

Change each mixed number to an improper fraction.

1. $3\frac{1}{2} = \frac{7}{2}$ 2. $4\frac{3}{8} = \frac{35}{8}$ 3. $6\frac{5}{7} = \frac{47}{7}$

4. $5\frac{7}{8} = \frac{47}{8}$ 5. $8\frac{2}{3} = \frac{26}{3}$ 6. $10\frac{3}{5} = \frac{53}{5}$

7. $7\frac{4}{5} = \frac{39}{5}$ 8. $2\frac{2}{3} = \frac{8}{3}$ 9. $4\frac{5}{9} = \frac{41}{9}$

10. $1\frac{1}{10} = \frac{11}{10}$ 11. $2\frac{4}{9} = \frac{22}{9}$ 12. $12\frac{13}{15} = \frac{193}{15}$

13. $6\frac{5}{8} = \frac{53}{8}$ 14. $4\frac{3}{4} = \frac{19}{4}$ 15. $3\frac{1}{3} = \frac{10}{3}$

16. $5\frac{2}{3} = \frac{17}{3}$ 17. $2\frac{3}{8} = \frac{19}{8}$ 18. $4\frac{2}{3} = \frac{14}{3}$

19. $9\frac{1}{2} = \frac{19}{2}$ 20. $4\frac{2}{4} = \frac{18}{4}$ 21. $6\frac{1}{5} = \frac{31}{5}$

Total Problems 21 Problems Correct ____

Worksheet 39

Name_____ Skill: Changing Mixed Numbers to Improper Fractions

Change each mixed number to an improper fraction.

1. $1\frac{2}{3} = \frac{5}{3}$ 2. $9\frac{6}{8} = \frac{78}{8}$ 3. $15\frac{3}{4} = \frac{63}{4}$

4. $10\frac{5}{6} = \frac{65}{6}$ 5. $9\frac{2}{8} = \frac{74}{8}$ 6. $7\frac{10}{16} = \frac{122}{16}$

7. $5\frac{4}{5} = \frac{29}{5}$ 8. $20\frac{2}{8} = \frac{162}{8}$ 9. $11\frac{3}{9} = \frac{102}{9}$

10. $2\frac{1}{12} = \frac{25}{12}$ 11. $8\frac{3}{9} = \frac{75}{9}$ 12. $7\frac{5}{6} = \frac{47}{6}$

13. $12\frac{4}{5} = \frac{64}{5}$ 14. $3\frac{3}{8} = \frac{27}{8}$ 15. $3\frac{2}{5} = \frac{17}{5}$

16. $1\frac{1}{5} = \frac{6}{5}$ 17. $2\frac{3}{4} = \frac{11}{4}$ 18. $6\frac{1}{3} = \frac{19}{3}$

19. $7\frac{1}{6} = \frac{43}{6}$ 20. $1\frac{1}{4} = \frac{5}{4}$ 21. $7\frac{2}{5} = \frac{37}{5}$

Total Problems 21 Problems Correct ____

Worksheet 40

Name_____ Skill: Making Fractions Equivalent

Make each pair of fractions equivalent.

1. $\frac{2}{3} = \frac{8}{12}$ 2. $\frac{3}{4} = \frac{12}{16}$ 3. $\frac{2}{5} = \frac{4}{10}$ 4. $\frac{1}{6} = \frac{2}{12}$

5. $\frac{8}{9} = \frac{48}{54}$ 6. $\frac{1}{2} = \frac{6}{12}$ 7. $\frac{3}{8} = \frac{6}{16}$ 8. $\frac{4}{5} = \frac{16}{20}$

9. $\frac{1}{2} = \frac{5}{10}$ 10. $\frac{4}{5} = \frac{20}{25}$ 11. $\frac{5}{8} = \frac{15}{24}$ 12. $\frac{3}{7} = \frac{9}{21}$

13. $\frac{1}{8} = \frac{4}{32}$ 14. $\frac{2}{5} = \frac{12}{30}$ 15. $\frac{3}{4} = \frac{18}{24}$ 16. $\frac{5}{6} = \frac{35}{42}$

17. $\frac{4}{9} = \frac{36}{81}$ 18. $\frac{7}{8} = \frac{56}{64}$ 19. $\frac{3}{5} = \frac{9}{15}$ 20. $\frac{1}{6} = \frac{6}{36}$

21. $\frac{2}{9} = \frac{4}{18}$ 22. $\frac{2}{3} = \frac{10}{15}$ 23. $\frac{3}{7} = \frac{6}{14}$ 24. $\frac{5}{8} = \frac{25}{40}$

Total Problems 24 Problems Correct ____

Answer Key

Worksheet 1 (page 41)

Name_____ Skill: Making Fractions Equivalent

Complete each row by filling in the numerators, making each fraction equivalent to the first one.

1. $\frac{3}{4} = \frac{18}{24} = \frac{12}{16} = \frac{6}{8} = \frac{15}{20} = \frac{27}{36}$

2. $\frac{1}{3} = \frac{3}{9} = \frac{9}{27} = \frac{30}{90} = \frac{2}{6} = \frac{4}{12}$

3. $\frac{2}{5} = \frac{20}{50} = \frac{4}{10} = \frac{16}{40} = \frac{6}{15} = \frac{10}{25}$

4. $\frac{1}{2} = \frac{18}{36} = \frac{9}{18} = \frac{8}{16} = \frac{21}{42} = \frac{24}{48}$

5. $\frac{7}{8} = \frac{14}{16} = \frac{49}{56} = \frac{21}{24} = \frac{42}{48} = \frac{28}{32}$

6. $\frac{3}{7} = \frac{9}{21} = \frac{18}{42} = \frac{6}{14} = \frac{15}{35} = \frac{12}{28}$

7. $\frac{4}{9} = \frac{8}{18} = \frac{20}{45} = \frac{16}{36} = \frac{24}{54} = \frac{12}{27}$

8. $\frac{5}{6} = \frac{40}{48} = \frac{10}{12} = \frac{25}{30} = \frac{15}{18} = \frac{20}{24}$

Total Problems __8__ Problems Correct ____

© Carson-Dellosa CD-3747
41

Worksheet 2 (page 42)

Name_____ Skill: Making Fractions and Whole Numbers Equivalent

Make each equivalent.

1. $4 = \frac{12}{3}$ 2. $\frac{1}{2} = \frac{4}{8}$ 3. $\frac{1}{3} = \frac{2}{6}$ 4. $\frac{2}{5} = \frac{4}{10}$

5. $6 = \frac{30}{5}$ 6. $4 = \frac{8}{2}$ 7. $\frac{5}{6} = \frac{20}{24}$ 8. $\frac{7}{8} = \frac{56}{64}$

9. $\frac{2}{3} = \frac{12}{18}$ 10. $3 = \frac{6}{2}$ 11. $2 = \frac{8}{4}$ 12. $\frac{2}{3} = \frac{10}{15}$

13. $\frac{1}{5} = \frac{4}{20}$ 14. $\frac{5}{8} = \frac{25}{40}$ 15. $\frac{1}{4} = \frac{4}{16}$ 16. $\frac{3}{5} = \frac{9}{15}$

17. $\frac{5}{6} = \frac{40}{48}$ 18. $\frac{1}{3} = \frac{12}{36}$ 19. $\frac{1}{8} = \frac{8}{64}$ 20. $\frac{3}{4} = \frac{18}{24}$

21. $\frac{1}{6} = \frac{6}{36}$ 22. $\frac{2}{7} = \frac{14}{49}$ 23. $\frac{2}{5} = \frac{12}{30}$ 24. $\frac{7}{8} = \frac{49}{56}$

Total Problems __24__ Problems Correct ____

© Carson-Dellosa CD-3747
42

Worksheet 3 (page 43)

Name_____ Skill: Adding Fractions with the Same Denominators

Add the fractions and write the answers in simplest form.

1. $\frac{1}{3} + \frac{2}{3} = 1$ 2. $\frac{1}{2} + \frac{1}{2} = 1$ 3. $\frac{3}{5} + \frac{2}{5} = 1$

4. $\frac{2}{9} + \frac{5}{9} = \frac{7}{9}$ 5. $\frac{5}{8} + \frac{3}{8} = 1$ 6. $\frac{3}{7} + \frac{2}{7} = \frac{5}{7}$

7. $\frac{1}{6} + \frac{1}{6} = \frac{1}{3}$ 8. $\frac{5}{5} + \frac{2}{5} = 1\frac{2}{5}$ 9. $\frac{1}{3} + \frac{2}{3} = 1$

10. $\frac{3}{6} + \frac{1}{6} = \frac{2}{3}$ 11. $\frac{2}{10} + \frac{4}{10} = \frac{3}{5}$ 12. $\frac{1}{7} + \frac{1}{7} = \frac{2}{7}$

13. $\frac{2}{4} + \frac{2}{4} = 1$ 14. $\frac{1}{2} + \frac{1}{2} = 1$ 15. $\frac{1}{6} + \frac{4}{6} = \frac{5}{6}$

Total Problems __15__ Problems Correct ____

© Carson-Dellosa CD-3747
43

Worksheet 4 (page 44)

Name_____ Skill: Adding Fractions with the Same Denominators

Add the fractions and write the answers in simplest form.

1. $\frac{2}{7} + \frac{3}{7} = \frac{5}{7}$ 2. $\frac{1}{5} + \frac{3}{5} = \frac{4}{5}$ 3. $\frac{4}{8} + \frac{2}{8} = \frac{3}{4}$ 4. $\frac{2}{10} + \frac{4}{10} = \frac{3}{4}$ 5. $\frac{2}{6} + \frac{1}{6} = \frac{1}{2}$

6. $\frac{6}{8} + \frac{1}{8} = \frac{7}{8}$ 7. $\frac{3}{5} + \frac{3}{5} = \frac{1}{5}$ 8. $\frac{6}{7} + \frac{5}{7} = \frac{4}{7}$ 9. $\frac{3}{4} + \frac{2}{4} = \frac{1}{4}$ 10. $\frac{2}{9} + \frac{1}{9} = \frac{1}{3}$

11. $\frac{7}{10} + \frac{9}{10} = \frac{3}{5}$ 12. $\frac{1}{4} + \frac{2}{4} = \frac{3}{4}$ 13. $\frac{1}{8} + \frac{5}{8} = \frac{3}{4}$ 14. $\frac{2}{3} + \frac{1}{3} = 1$ 15. $\frac{5}{12} + \frac{5}{12} = \frac{5}{6}$

16. $\frac{3}{7} + \frac{1}{7} = \frac{4}{7}$ 17. $\frac{1}{5} + \frac{3}{5} = \frac{4}{5}$ 18. $\frac{2}{8} + \frac{4}{8} = \frac{3}{4}$ 19. $\frac{4}{9} + \frac{3}{9} = \frac{7}{9}$ 20. $\frac{1}{6} + \frac{3}{6} = \frac{2}{3}$

Total Problems __20__ Problems Correct ____

© Carson-Dellosa CD-3747
44

Answer Key

Worksheet 1 (page 45)

Name_____

Skill: Adding Mixed Numbers with the Same Denominators

Add and write the answers in simplest form.

1. $1\frac{2}{5} + 2\frac{3}{5} = 4$
2. $6\frac{5}{8} + 7\frac{2}{8} = 13\frac{7}{8}$
3. $2\frac{3}{4} + 2\frac{1}{4} = 5$

4. $5\frac{2}{7} + 6\frac{4}{7} = 11\frac{6}{7}$
5. $3\frac{3}{8} + 4\frac{1}{8} = 7\frac{1}{2}$
6. $5\frac{11}{15} + 6\frac{10}{15} = 12\frac{6}{15}$

7. $3\frac{3}{8} + 4\frac{1}{8} = 7\frac{1}{2}$
8. $8\frac{2}{5} + 1\frac{2}{5} = 9\frac{4}{5}$
9. $2\frac{2}{5} + 2\frac{2}{5} = 4\frac{4}{5}$

10. $4\frac{2}{9} + 5\frac{3}{9} = 9\frac{5}{9}$
11. $7\frac{1}{8} + 7\frac{1}{8} = 14\frac{1}{4}$
12. $4\frac{3}{4} + 1\frac{1}{4} = 6$

Total Problems _12_ Problems Correct ____

45

Worksheet 2 (page 46)

Name_____

Skill: Adding Mixed Numbers with the Same Denominators

Add and write the answers in simplest form.

1. $4\frac{5}{8} + 5\frac{4}{8} = 10\frac{1}{8}$
2. $1\frac{1}{2} + 4\frac{1}{2} = 6$
3. $6\frac{2}{3} + 7\frac{2}{3} = 14\frac{1}{3}$
4. $3\frac{9}{10} + 7\frac{6}{10} = 11\frac{1}{2}$

5. $2\frac{2}{5} + 6\frac{4}{5} = 9\frac{1}{5}$
6. $8\frac{4}{9} + 1\frac{5}{9} = 10$
7. $4\frac{2}{7} + 5\frac{3}{7} = 9\frac{5}{7}$
8. $3\frac{1}{3} + 4\frac{2}{3} = 8$

9. $4\frac{5}{8} + 5\frac{4}{8} = 10\frac{1}{8}$
10. $8\frac{4}{9} + 1\frac{5}{9} = 10$
11. $4\frac{2}{7} + 6\frac{3}{7} = 10\frac{5}{7}$
12. $3\frac{1}{3} + 4\frac{2}{3} = 8$

13. $10\frac{3}{4} + 8\frac{2}{4} = 19\frac{1}{4}$
14. $2\frac{5}{6} + 8\frac{5}{6} = 11\frac{2}{3}$
15. $9\frac{4}{12} + 6\frac{10}{12} = 16\frac{1}{6}$
16. $1\frac{4}{5} + 5\frac{3}{5} = 7\frac{2}{5}$

Total Problems _16_ Problems Correct ____

46

Worksheet 3 (page 47)

Name_____

Skill: Adding Fractions with Different Denominators

Add and write the answers in simplest form.

1. $\frac{7}{8} + \frac{1}{4} = 1\frac{1}{8}$
2. $\frac{3}{10} + \frac{4}{5} = 1\frac{1}{10}$
3. $\frac{1}{4} + \frac{1}{2} = \frac{3}{4}$
4. $\frac{1}{10} + \frac{4}{8} = \frac{3}{5}$
5. $\frac{2}{3} + \frac{5}{6} = 1\frac{1}{2}$

6. $\frac{1}{3} + \frac{5}{6} = 1\frac{1}{6}$
7. $\frac{1}{12} + \frac{3}{4} = \frac{5}{6}$
8. $\frac{2}{3} + \frac{4}{9} = 1\frac{1}{9}$
9. $\frac{5}{8} + \frac{1}{2} = 1\frac{1}{8}$
10. $\frac{5}{12} + \frac{1}{4} = \frac{2}{3}$

11. $\frac{5}{12} + \frac{1}{10} = \frac{31}{60}$
12. $\frac{2}{5} + \frac{5}{10} = \frac{9}{10}$
13. $\frac{1}{8} + \frac{5}{9} = \frac{49}{72}$
14. $\frac{2}{3} + \frac{1}{6} = \frac{5}{6}$
15. $\frac{6}{12} + \frac{7}{13} = 1\frac{1}{26}$

16. $\frac{2}{7} + \frac{1}{5} = \frac{17}{35}$
17. $\frac{4}{5} + \frac{3}{6} = 1\frac{3}{10}$
18. $\frac{2}{7} + \frac{1}{3} = \frac{13}{21}$
19. $\frac{4}{8} + \frac{3}{7} = \frac{13}{14}$
20. $\frac{1}{2} + \frac{3}{4} = 1\frac{1}{4}$

Total Problems _20_ Problems Correct ____

47

Worksheet 4 (page 48)

Name_____

Skill: Adding Fractions with Different Denominators

Add and write the answers in simplest form.

1. $\frac{2}{5} + \frac{1}{2} = \frac{9}{10}$
2. $\frac{3}{10} + \frac{1}{3} = \frac{19}{20}$
3. $\frac{7}{8} + \frac{1}{3} = 1\frac{5}{24}$
4. $\frac{2}{10} + \frac{3}{4} = \frac{19}{20}$
5. $\frac{2}{3} + \frac{4}{5} = 1\frac{7}{15}$

6. $\frac{2}{3} + \frac{3}{4} = 1\frac{5}{12}$
7. $\frac{1}{3} + \frac{2}{5} = \frac{11}{15}$
8. $\frac{5}{6} + \frac{2}{5} = 1\frac{7}{30}$
9. $\frac{5}{6} + \frac{1}{4} = 1\frac{1}{12}$
10. $\frac{3}{12} + \frac{2}{4} = \frac{3}{4}$

11. $\frac{6}{12} + \frac{3}{10} = \frac{4}{5}$
12. $\frac{2}{6} + \frac{5}{12} = \frac{3}{4}$
13. $\frac{1}{7} + \frac{5}{8} = \frac{43}{56}$
14. $\frac{1}{4} + \frac{2}{5} = \frac{13}{20}$
15. $\frac{5}{13} + \frac{7}{12} = \frac{151}{156}$

16. $\frac{2}{6} + \frac{1}{8} = \frac{11}{24}$
17. $\frac{4}{8} + \frac{3}{5} = 1\frac{1}{10}$
18. $\frac{2}{9} + \frac{2}{3} = \frac{8}{9}$
19. $\frac{2}{4} + \frac{3}{7} = \frac{13}{14}$
20. $\frac{1}{3} + \frac{3}{6} = \frac{5}{6}$

Total Problems _20_ Problems Correct ____

48

107

Answer Key

Name_____

Skill: Adding Mixed Numbers with Different Denominators

Add and write the answers in simplest form.

1. $4\frac{5}{8} + 3\frac{1}{6} = 7\frac{19}{24}$
2. $3\frac{2}{5} + 2\frac{1}{2} = 5\frac{9}{10}$
3. $1\frac{7}{9} + 4\frac{1}{5} = 5\frac{44}{45}$
4. $6\frac{3}{10} + 7\frac{1}{3} = 13\frac{19}{30}$

5. $2\frac{5}{6} + 6\frac{3}{4} = 9\frac{7}{12}$
6. $8\frac{5}{7} + 9\frac{2}{3} = 18\frac{8}{21}$
7. $6\frac{5}{6} + 2\frac{2}{3} = 9\frac{1}{2}$
8. $5\frac{4}{5} + 3\frac{2}{3} = 9\frac{7}{15}$

9. $4\frac{5}{8} + 5\frac{4}{12} = 9\frac{23}{24}$
10. $8\frac{2}{3} + 1\frac{5}{9} = 10\frac{2}{9}$
11. $4\frac{2}{14} + 6\frac{3}{7} = 10\frac{4}{7}$
12. $3\frac{1}{6} + 4\frac{2}{3} = 7\frac{5}{6}$

13. $10\frac{3}{8} + 3\frac{1}{2} = 13\frac{7}{8}$
14. $2\frac{3}{4} + 7\frac{1}{2} = 10\frac{1}{4}$
15. $1\frac{1}{4} + 5\frac{10}{12} = 7\frac{1}{12}$
16. $9\frac{1}{2} + 8\frac{3}{7} = 17\frac{13}{14}$

Total Problems __16__ Problems Correct ____

49

Name_____

Skill: Adding Mixed Numbers with Different Denominators

Add and write the answers in simplest form.

1. $1\frac{3}{8} + 2\frac{1}{2} = 3\frac{7}{8}$
2. $5\frac{2}{5} + 3\frac{1}{3} = 8\frac{11}{15}$
3. $5\frac{3}{4} + 6\frac{5}{6} = 12\frac{7}{12}$
4. $4\frac{7}{12} + 5\frac{1}{2} = 10\frac{1}{12}$

5. $3\frac{11}{12} + 4\frac{1}{2} = 8\frac{5}{12}$
6. $2\frac{4}{9} + 5\frac{1}{3} = 7\frac{7}{9}$
7. $1\frac{3}{4} + 3\frac{2}{3} = 5\frac{5}{12}$
8. $10\frac{5}{8} + 2\frac{2}{3} = 13\frac{7}{24}$

9. $6\frac{5}{6} + 4\frac{2}{3} = 11\frac{1}{2}$
10. $2\frac{2}{7} + 1\frac{1}{3} = 3\frac{13}{21}$
11. $4\frac{3}{5} + 5\frac{1}{4} = 9\frac{17}{20}$
12. $12\frac{3}{4} + 8\frac{2}{5} = 21\frac{3}{20}$

13. $7\frac{2}{3} + 8\frac{4}{5} = 16\frac{7}{15}$
14. $2\frac{7}{8} + 4\frac{5}{6} = 7\frac{17}{24}$
15. $1\frac{5}{7} + 4\frac{3}{12} = 5\frac{27}{28}$
16. $9\frac{1}{8} + 6\frac{3}{4} = 15\frac{7}{8}$

Total Problems __16__ Problems Correct ____

50

Name_____

Skill: Adding Fractions and Mixed Numbers Review

Add and write the answers in simplest form.

1. $2\frac{1}{3} + 4\frac{1}{3} = 6\frac{2}{3}$
2. $6\frac{1}{9} + 3\frac{2}{9} = 9\frac{1}{3}$
3. $1\frac{1}{6} + 2\frac{3}{8} = 3\frac{13}{24}$

4. $2\frac{3}{4} + 7\frac{1}{3} = 10\frac{1}{12}$
5. $1\frac{3}{8} + 2\frac{1}{3} = 3\frac{17}{24}$
6. $4\frac{10}{12} + 6\frac{11}{15} = 11\frac{17}{30}$

7. $\frac{1}{8} + \frac{1}{4} = \frac{3}{8}$
8. $\frac{2}{5} + \frac{1}{5} = \frac{3}{5}$
9. $\frac{3}{3} + \frac{1}{7} = 1\frac{1}{7}$
10. $\frac{1}{2} + \frac{2}{3} = 1\frac{1}{6}$

11. $\frac{3}{7} + \frac{1}{2} = \frac{13}{14}$
12. $\frac{4}{7} + \frac{1}{7} = \frac{5}{7}$
13. $\frac{3}{9} + \frac{2}{5} = \frac{11}{15}$
14. $\frac{4}{6} + \frac{2}{6} = 1$

15. $\frac{2}{9} + \frac{2}{7} = \frac{32}{63}$
16. $\frac{5}{7} + \frac{2}{6} = 1\frac{1}{21}$
17. $\frac{4}{9} + \frac{9}{9} = 1\frac{2}{3}$
18. $\frac{2}{3} + \frac{1}{5} = \frac{13}{15}$

Total Problems __18__ Problems Correct ____

51

Name_____

Skill: Adding Fractions and Mixed Numbers Review

Add and write the answers in simplest form.

1. $\frac{2}{3} + \frac{1}{5} = \frac{13}{15}$
2. $\frac{2}{10} + \frac{3}{5} = \frac{4}{5}$
3. $\frac{2}{7} + \frac{5}{7} = 1$
4. $\frac{3}{11} + \frac{4}{8} = \frac{17}{22}$
5. $\frac{3}{4} + \frac{1}{4} = 1$

6. $\frac{4}{5} + \frac{7}{8} = \frac{27}{40}$
7. $\frac{1}{10} + \frac{3}{5} = \frac{7}{10}$
8. $\frac{4}{5} + \frac{1}{8} = \frac{37}{40}$
9. $\frac{2}{7} + \frac{1}{9} = \frac{25}{63}$
10. $\frac{2}{12} + \frac{1}{8} = \frac{7}{24}$

11. $8\frac{1}{3} + 1\frac{1}{3} = 9\frac{2}{3}$
12. $2\frac{4}{8} + 6\frac{5}{6} = 9\frac{1}{3}$
13. $4\frac{2}{7} + 6\frac{3}{7} = 10\frac{5}{7}$
14. $2\frac{1}{3} + 4\frac{2}{5} = 6\frac{11}{15}$

15. $11\frac{2}{3} + 9\frac{1}{5} = 20\frac{13}{15}$
16. $3\frac{1}{6} + 2\frac{3}{6} = 5\frac{2}{3}$
17. $8\frac{3}{10} + 3\frac{10}{11} = 12\frac{23}{110}$
18. $1\frac{4}{6} + 5\frac{3}{6} = 7\frac{1}{6}$

Total Problems __18__ Problems Correct ____

52

Answer Key

Page 53

Name_____ Skill: Subtracting Fractions with the Same Denominators

Subtract the fractions and write the answers in simplest form.

1. $\frac{5}{6} - \frac{1}{6} = \frac{2}{3}$
2. $\frac{7}{8} - \frac{3}{8} = \frac{1}{2}$
3. $\frac{3}{10} - \frac{1}{10} = \frac{1}{5}$
4. $\frac{15}{16} - \frac{11}{16} = \frac{1}{4}$
5. $\frac{3}{4} - \frac{1}{4} = \frac{1}{2}$

6. $\frac{7}{12} - \frac{5}{12} = \frac{1}{6}$
7. $\frac{5}{7} - \frac{2}{7} = \frac{3}{7}$
8. $\frac{7}{9} - \frac{1}{9} = \frac{2}{3}$
9. $\frac{4}{5} - \frac{2}{5} = \frac{2}{5}$
10. $\frac{13}{15} - \frac{11}{15} = \frac{2}{15}$

11. $\frac{9}{14} - \frac{1}{14} = \frac{4}{7}$
12. $\frac{9}{11} - \frac{1}{11} = \frac{8}{11}$
13. $\frac{5}{8} - \frac{1}{8} = \frac{1}{2}$
14. $\frac{2}{3} - \frac{1}{3} = \frac{1}{3}$
15. $\frac{9}{10} - \frac{7}{10} = \frac{1}{5}$

16. $\frac{7}{8} - \frac{5}{8} = \frac{1}{4}$
17. $\frac{5}{9} - \frac{4}{9} = \frac{1}{9}$
18. $\frac{5}{7} - \frac{3}{7} = \frac{2}{7}$
19. $\frac{2}{5} - \frac{1}{5} = \frac{1}{5}$
20. $\frac{3}{3} - \frac{1}{3} = \frac{2}{3}$

Total Problems 20 Problems Correct ____

53

Page 54

Name_____ Skill: Subtracting Fractions with the Same Denominators

Subtract the fractions and write the answers in simplest form.

1. $\frac{2}{5} - \frac{1}{5} = \frac{1}{5}$
2. $\frac{7}{9} - \frac{3}{9} = \frac{4}{9}$
3. $\frac{3}{8} - \frac{2}{8} = \frac{1}{8}$

4. $\frac{5}{9} - \frac{2}{9} = \frac{1}{3}$
5. $\frac{5}{10} - \frac{2}{10} = \frac{3}{10}$
6. $\frac{2}{3} - \frac{1}{3} = \frac{1}{3}$

7. $\frac{6}{7} - \frac{1}{7} = \frac{5}{7}$
8. $\frac{5}{5} - \frac{2}{5} = \frac{3}{5}$
9. $\frac{3}{4} - \frac{2}{4} = \frac{1}{4}$

10. $\frac{5}{6} - \frac{3}{6} = \frac{1}{3}$
11. $\frac{9}{20} - \frac{2}{20} = \frac{7}{20}$
12. $\frac{1}{7} - \frac{1}{7} = 0$

13. $\frac{2}{9} - \frac{2}{9} = 0$
14. $\frac{2}{2} - \frac{1}{2} = \frac{1}{2}$
15. $\frac{1}{1} - \frac{1}{1} = 0$

Total Problems 15 Problems Correct ____

54

Page 55

Name_____ Skill: Subtracting Fractions from Whole Numbers

Subtract and write the answers in simplest form.

1. $2 - \frac{7}{8} = 1\frac{1}{8}$
2. $4 - \frac{3}{5} = 3\frac{2}{5}$
3. $3 - \frac{3}{4} = 2\frac{1}{4}$
4. $8 - \frac{9}{9} = 7$
5. $7 - \frac{4}{5} = 6\frac{1}{5}$

6. $4 - \frac{3}{10} = 3\frac{7}{10}$
7. $5 - \frac{6}{9} = 4\frac{1}{3}$
8. $4 - \frac{3}{6} = 3\frac{1}{2}$
9. $5 - \frac{2}{5} = 4\frac{3}{5}$
10. $10 - \frac{1}{2} = 9\frac{1}{2}$

11. $12 - \frac{5}{7} = 11\frac{2}{7}$
12. $9 - \frac{1}{3} = 8\frac{2}{3}$
13. $4 - \frac{7}{8} = 3\frac{1}{8}$
14. $3 - \frac{6}{7} = 2\frac{1}{7}$
15. $6 - \frac{1}{6} = 5\frac{5}{6}$

16. $5 - \frac{1}{4} = 4\frac{3}{4}$
17. $4 - \frac{2}{6} = 3\frac{2}{3}$
18. $3 - \frac{2}{3} = 2\frac{1}{3}$
19. $2 - \frac{6}{8} = 1\frac{1}{4}$
20. $1 - \frac{3}{5} = \frac{2}{5}$

Total Problems 20 Problems Correct ____

55

Page 56

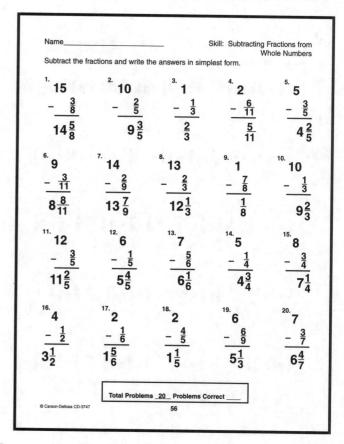

Name_____ Skill: Subtracting Fractions from Whole Numbers

Subtract the fractions and write the answers in simplest form.

1. $15 - \frac{3}{8} = 14\frac{5}{8}$
2. $10 - \frac{2}{5} = 9\frac{3}{5}$
3. $1 - \frac{1}{3} = \frac{2}{3}$
4. $2 - \frac{6}{11} = \frac{5}{11}$
5. $5 - \frac{3}{5} = 4\frac{2}{5}$

6. $9 - \frac{3}{11} = 8\frac{8}{11}$
7. $14 - \frac{2}{9} = 13\frac{7}{9}$
8. $13 - \frac{2}{3} = 12\frac{1}{3}$
9. $1 - \frac{7}{8} = \frac{1}{8}$
10. $10 - \frac{1}{3} = 9\frac{2}{3}$

11. $12 - \frac{3}{5} = 11\frac{2}{5}$
12. $6 - \frac{1}{5} = 5\frac{4}{5}$
13. $7 - \frac{5}{6} = 6\frac{1}{6}$
14. $5 - \frac{1}{4} = 4\frac{3}{4}$
15. $8 - \frac{3}{4} = 7\frac{1}{4}$

16. $4 - \frac{1}{2} = 3\frac{1}{2}$
17. $2 - \frac{1}{6} = 1\frac{5}{6}$
18. $2 - \frac{4}{5} = 1\frac{1}{5}$
19. $6 - \frac{6}{9} = 5\frac{1}{3}$
20. $7 - \frac{3}{7} = 6\frac{4}{7}$

Total Problems 20 Problems Correct ____

56

Answer Key

Worksheet 57

Subtract and write the answers in simplest form.

1. $5\frac{5}{8} - 2\frac{4}{8} = 3\frac{1}{8}$
2. $8\frac{4}{5} - 4\frac{1}{5} = 4\frac{3}{5}$
3. $5\frac{2}{3} - 1\frac{1}{3} = 4\frac{1}{3}$
4. $3\frac{2}{10} - 1\frac{2}{10} = 2$

5. $4\frac{2}{6} - 3\frac{5}{6} = \frac{1}{2}$
6. $3\frac{2}{6} - 2\frac{1}{6} = 1\frac{1}{6}$
7. $10\frac{3}{4} - 7\frac{1}{4} = 3\frac{1}{2}$
8. $6\frac{7}{8} - 1\frac{1}{8} = 5\frac{3}{4}$

9. $5\frac{5}{8} - 3\frac{4}{8} = 2\frac{1}{8}$
10. $9\frac{6}{7} - 2\frac{2}{7} = 7\frac{4}{7}$
11. $5\frac{3}{3} - 4\frac{2}{3} = 1\frac{1}{3}$
12. $2\frac{1}{8} - 1\frac{1}{8} = 1$

13. $7\frac{3}{5} - 5\frac{1}{5} = 2\frac{2}{5}$
14. $8\frac{7}{9} - 8\frac{6}{9} = \frac{1}{9}$
15. $4\frac{9}{10} - 2\frac{7}{10} = 2\frac{1}{5}$
16. $2\frac{3}{5} - 1\frac{4}{5} = \frac{4}{5}$

Total Problems _16_ Problems Correct ____

57

Worksheet 58

Subtract and write the answers in simplest form.

1. $12\frac{7}{8} - 5\frac{5}{8} = 7\frac{1}{4}$
2. $10\frac{2}{5} - 7\frac{4}{5} = 2\frac{3}{5}$
3. $5\frac{2}{3} - 1\frac{1}{3} = 4\frac{1}{3}$
4. $6\frac{2}{12} - 3\frac{2}{12} = 3$

5. $2\frac{2}{3} - 2\frac{1}{3} = \frac{1}{3}$
6. $3\frac{1}{4} - 2\frac{3}{4} = \frac{1}{2}$
7. $8\frac{7}{10} - 7\frac{9}{10} = \frac{4}{5}$
8. $4\frac{5}{6} - 2\frac{1}{6} = 2\frac{2}{3}$

9. $9\frac{7}{8} - 4\frac{4}{8} = 5\frac{3}{8}$
10. $10\frac{2}{3} - 9\frac{1}{3} = 1\frac{1}{3}$
11. $8\frac{3}{16} - 7\frac{5}{16} = \frac{7}{8}$
12. $4\frac{11}{18} - 1\frac{7}{18} = 3\frac{2}{9}$

13. $3\frac{1}{8} - 1\frac{7}{8} = 1\frac{1}{4}$
14. $5\frac{4}{5} - 4\frac{1}{5} = 1\frac{3}{5}$
15. $6\frac{7}{15} - 2\frac{8}{15} = 3\frac{14}{15}$
16. $8\frac{7}{10} - 1\frac{3}{10} = 7\frac{2}{5}$

Total Problems _16_ Problems Correct ____

58

Worksheet 59

Subtract the fractions and write the answers in simplest form.

1. $\frac{1}{3} - \frac{1}{4} = \frac{1}{12}$
2. $\frac{3}{5} - \frac{1}{3} = \frac{4}{15}$
3. $\frac{7}{12} - \frac{1}{4} = \frac{1}{3}$
4. $\frac{2}{3} - \frac{1}{2} = \frac{1}{6}$
5. $\frac{5}{6} - \frac{1}{5} = \frac{19}{30}$

6. $\frac{3}{4} - \frac{1}{5} = \frac{11}{20}$
7. $\frac{3}{8} - \frac{2}{6} = \frac{1}{24}$
8. $\frac{3}{9} - \frac{1}{4} = \frac{1}{12}$
9. $\frac{2}{3} - \frac{4}{9} = \frac{2}{9}$
10. $\frac{7}{8} - \frac{3}{10} = \frac{23}{40}$

11. $\frac{9}{10} - \frac{5}{7} = \frac{13}{70}$
12. $\frac{2}{4} - \frac{1}{3} = \frac{1}{6}$
13. $\frac{7}{8} - \frac{1}{9} = \frac{55}{72}$
14. $\frac{1}{3} - \frac{1}{6} = \frac{1}{6}$
15. $\frac{9}{12} - \frac{1}{11} = \frac{75}{132}$

16. $\frac{5}{7} - \frac{2}{9} = \frac{1}{3}$
17. $\frac{1}{5} - \frac{1}{8} = \frac{3}{40}$
18. $\frac{8}{8} - \frac{4}{6} = \frac{1}{3}$
19. $\frac{8}{9} - \frac{3}{6} = \frac{7}{17}$
20. $\frac{6}{6} - \frac{3}{12} = \frac{3}{4}$

Total Problems _20_ Problems Correct ____

59

Worksheet 60

Subtract the fractions and write the answers in simplest form.

1. $\frac{3}{4} - \frac{1}{6} = \frac{7}{12}$
2. $\frac{5}{6} - \frac{2}{5} = \frac{13}{30}$
3. $\frac{11}{12} - \frac{1}{6} = \frac{3}{4}$
4. $\frac{5}{12} - \frac{1}{3} = \frac{1}{12}$
5. $\frac{3}{4} - \frac{1}{3} = \frac{5}{12}$

6. $\frac{13}{15} - \frac{2}{3} = \frac{1}{5}$
7. $\frac{2}{3} - \frac{1}{6} = \frac{1}{2}$
8. $\frac{5}{6} - \frac{3}{7} = \frac{17}{42}$
9. $\frac{7}{8} - \frac{1}{6} = \frac{17}{24}$
10. $\frac{8}{9} - \frac{5}{6} = \frac{1}{18}$

11. $\frac{2}{3} - \frac{7}{12} = \frac{1}{12}$
12. $\frac{11}{14} - \frac{1}{2} = \frac{4}{7}$
13. $\frac{7}{8} - \frac{1}{9} = \frac{55}{72}$
14. $\frac{1}{3} - \frac{1}{6} = \frac{1}{6}$
15. $\frac{9}{12} - \frac{2}{11} = \frac{75}{132}$

16. $\frac{5}{6} - \frac{1}{3} = \frac{1}{2}$
17. $\frac{7}{12} - \frac{1}{4} = \frac{1}{3}$
18. $\frac{7}{8} - \frac{1}{2} = \frac{3}{8}$
19. $\frac{2}{3} - \frac{4}{9} = \frac{2}{9}$
20. $\frac{5}{6} - \frac{1}{8} = \frac{17}{24}$

Total Problems _20_ Problems Correct ____

60

Answer Key

Name_____ Skill: Subtracting Mixed Numbers with Different Denominators

Subtract and write the answers in simplest form.

1. $2\frac{2}{3} - 1\frac{1}{2} = 1\frac{1}{6}$

2. $4\frac{7}{10} - 1\frac{2}{5} = 3\frac{3}{10}$

3. $4\frac{1}{3} - 1\frac{2}{5} = 2\frac{14}{15}$

4. $6\frac{2}{7} - 4\frac{1}{2} = 1\frac{11}{14}$

5. $4\frac{1}{3} - 2\frac{3}{8} = 1\frac{23}{24}$

6. $3\frac{7}{8} - 2\frac{1}{6} = 1\frac{17}{24}$

7. $5\frac{5}{12} - 3\frac{7}{10} = 1\frac{43}{60}$

8. $4\frac{2}{5} - 2\frac{3}{10} = 2\frac{1}{10}$

9. $3\frac{5}{6} - 2\frac{1}{12} = 1\frac{3}{4}$

10. $5\frac{4}{9} - 2\frac{1}{3} = 3\frac{1}{9}$

11. $3\frac{5}{6} - 1\frac{5}{9} = 2\frac{5}{18}$

12. $6\frac{4}{5} - 5\frac{3}{7} = 1\frac{13}{35}$

13. $5\frac{5}{8} - 2\frac{3}{4} = 2\frac{7}{8}$

14. $3\frac{1}{2} - 1\frac{3}{4} = 1\frac{3}{4}$

15. $7\frac{3}{5} - 4\frac{7}{10} = 2\frac{9}{10}$

16. $4\frac{7}{8} - 2\frac{1}{4} = 2\frac{5}{8}$

Total Problems 16 Problems Correct ____

61

Name_____ Skill: Subtracting Mixed Numbers with Different Denominators

Subtract and write the answers in simplest form.

1. $5\frac{1}{6} - 2\frac{3}{4} = 2\frac{5}{12}$

2. $4\frac{1}{3} - 1\frac{1}{4} = 3\frac{1}{12}$

3. $6\frac{1}{2} - 1\frac{1}{3} = 5\frac{1}{6}$

4. $5\frac{1}{3} - 3\frac{3}{4} = 1\frac{7}{12}$

5. $4\frac{7}{10} - 1\frac{4}{5} = 2\frac{9}{10}$

6. $3\frac{7}{12} - 1\frac{9}{10} = 1\frac{41}{60}$

7. $7\frac{1}{4} - 3\frac{2}{3} = 3\frac{7}{12}$

8. $8\frac{2}{5} - 4\frac{1}{4} = 4\frac{3}{20}$

9. $5\frac{7}{8} - 1\frac{1}{16} = 4\frac{13}{16}$

10. $5\frac{4}{5} - 2\frac{1}{3} = 3\frac{7}{15}$

11. $10\frac{4}{5} - 6\frac{5}{6} = 3\frac{29}{30}$

12. $2\frac{2}{3} - 2\frac{1}{4} = \frac{5}{12}$

13. $3\frac{1}{3} - 1\frac{5}{6} = 1\frac{1}{2}$

14. $4\frac{3}{4} - 1\frac{5}{6} = 2\frac{11}{12}$

15. $12\frac{2}{3} - 9\frac{6}{7} = 2\frac{11}{21}$

16. $6\frac{1}{3} - 5\frac{3}{4} = \frac{7}{12}$

Total Problems 16 Problems Correct ____

62

Name_____ Skill: Multiplying Fractions

Multiply the fractions and write answers in simplest form.

1. $\frac{3}{4} \times \frac{2}{5} = \frac{3}{10}$

2. $\frac{1}{4} \times \frac{3}{5} = \frac{3}{20}$

3. $\frac{1}{8} \times \frac{2}{5} = \frac{1}{20}$

4. $\frac{7}{8} \times \frac{1}{6} = \frac{7}{48}$

5. $\frac{4}{7} \times \frac{3}{8} = \frac{3}{14}$

6. $\frac{1}{6} \times \frac{2}{3} = \frac{1}{9}$

7. $\frac{4}{5} \times \frac{2}{3} = \frac{8}{15}$

8. $\frac{2}{3} \times \frac{2}{5} = \frac{4}{15}$

9. $\frac{1}{2} \times \frac{3}{4} = \frac{3}{8}$

10. $\frac{1}{3} \times \frac{1}{5} = \frac{1}{15}$

11. $\frac{2}{3} \times \frac{4}{5} = \frac{8}{15}$

12. $\frac{1}{8} \times \frac{1}{3} = \frac{1}{24}$

13. $\frac{2}{7} \times \frac{2}{9} = \frac{4}{63}$

14. $\frac{3}{5} \times \frac{1}{3} = \frac{1}{5}$

15. $\frac{1}{6} \times \frac{4}{5} = \frac{2}{15}$

Total Problems 15 Problems Correct ____

63

Name_____ Skill: Multiplying Fractions

Multiply the fractions and write answers in simplest form.

1. $\frac{1}{3} \times \frac{1}{7} = \frac{1}{21}$

2. $\frac{1}{4} \times \frac{1}{6} = \frac{1}{24}$

3. $\frac{1}{5} \times \frac{5}{6} = \frac{1}{6}$

4. $\frac{3}{5} \times \frac{2}{9} = \frac{6}{45}$

5. $\frac{2}{3} \times \frac{3}{8} = \frac{1}{4}$

6. $\frac{1}{2} \times \frac{3}{7} = \frac{3}{14}$

7. $\frac{1}{6} \times \frac{4}{5} = \frac{2}{15}$

8. $\frac{3}{4} \times \frac{4}{7} = \frac{3}{7}$

9. $\frac{2}{5} \times \frac{4}{9} = \frac{8}{45}$

10. $\frac{2}{7} \times \frac{5}{8} = \frac{5}{28}$

11. $\frac{2}{5} \times \frac{5}{6} = \frac{1}{3}$

12. $\frac{2}{8} \times \frac{3}{3} = \frac{1}{4}$

13. $\frac{2}{5} \times \frac{4}{9} = \frac{8}{45}$

14. $\frac{4}{5} \times \frac{2}{3} = \frac{8}{15}$

15. $\frac{1}{7} \times \frac{6}{8} = \frac{3}{28}$

Total Problems 15 Problems Correct ____

64

Answer Key

Name_____   Skill: Multiplying Fractions and
                                      Whole Numbers

Multiply and write the answers in simplest form.

1. $4 \times \frac{1}{2} = 2$ 2. $\frac{2}{5} \times 3 = 1\frac{1}{5}$ 3. $\frac{1}{3} \times 7 = 2\frac{1}{3}$

4. $2 \times \frac{2}{5} = \frac{4}{5}$ 5. $\frac{1}{8} \times 5 = \frac{5}{8}$ 6. $4 \times \frac{3}{4} = 3$

7. $4 \times \frac{2}{7} = \frac{1}{7}$ 8. $\frac{5}{7} \times 5 = 3\frac{4}{7}$ 9. $\frac{6}{8} \times 2 = 1\frac{1}{2}$

10. $3 \times \frac{5}{6} = 2\frac{1}{2}$ 11. $\frac{2}{3} \times 2 = 1\frac{1}{3}$ 12. $5 \times \frac{4}{5} = 4$

13. $8 \times \frac{1}{8} = 1$ 14. $\frac{3}{9} \times 4 = 1\frac{1}{3}$ 15. $3 \times \frac{2}{3} = 2$

Total Problems _15_ Problems Correct ____

© Carson-Dellosa CD-3747
65

Name_____   Skill: Multiplying Fractions and
                                      Whole Numbers

Multiply and write the answers in simplest form.

1. $5 \times \frac{2}{5} = 2$ 2. $\frac{2}{3} \times 4 = 2\frac{2}{3}$ 3. $\frac{3}{4} \times 5 = 3\frac{3}{4}$

4. $8 \times \frac{1}{7} = 1\frac{1}{7}$ 5. $\frac{1}{9} \times 6 = \frac{2}{3}$ 6. $2 \times \frac{4}{5} = 1\frac{3}{5}$

7. $6 \times \frac{3}{8} = 2\frac{1}{4}$ 8. $\frac{5}{6} \times 4 = 3\frac{1}{3}$ 9. $\frac{2}{7} \times 6 = 1\frac{5}{7}$

10. $4 \times \frac{8}{9} = 3\frac{5}{9}$ 11. $\frac{4}{6} \times 3 = 2$ 12. $7 \times \frac{3}{5} = 4\frac{1}{5}$

13. $2 \times \frac{3}{7} = \frac{6}{7}$ 14. $\frac{4}{5} \times 6 = 4\frac{4}{5}$ 15. $7 \times \frac{5}{6} = 5\frac{5}{6}$

Total Problems _15_ Problems Correct ____

© Carson-Dellosa CD-3747
66

Name_____   Skill: Multiplying Fractions and
                                      Whole Numbers

Multiply and write the answers in simplest form.

1. $10 \times \frac{2}{3} = 6\frac{2}{3}$ 2. $9 \times \frac{5}{6} = 7\frac{1}{2}$ 3. $12 \times \frac{7}{8} = 10\frac{1}{2}$

4. $4 \times \frac{4}{7} = 2\frac{2}{7}$ 5. $3 \times \frac{1}{3} = 1$ 6. $5 \times \frac{3}{4} = 3\frac{3}{4}$

7. $7 \times \frac{10}{11} = 6\frac{4}{11}$ 8. $30 \times \frac{3}{90} = 1$ 9. $22 \times \frac{1}{44} = \frac{1}{2}$

10. $36 \times \frac{2}{288} = \frac{1}{4}$ 11. $12 \times \frac{1}{36} = \frac{1}{3}$ 12. $4 \times \frac{1}{8} = \frac{1}{2}$

13. $6 \times \frac{4}{8} = 3$ 14. $5 \times \frac{2}{5} = 2$ 15. $8 \times \frac{2}{3} = 5\frac{1}{3}$

Total Problems _15_ Problems Correct ____

© Carson-Dellosa CD-3747
67

Name_____   Skill: Multiplying Mixed Numbers
                                      and Whole Numbers

Multiply and write the answers in simplest form.

1. $2 \times 2\frac{1}{3} = 4\frac{2}{3}$ 2. $4 \times 5\frac{1}{8} = 20\frac{1}{2}$ 3. $7 \times 1\frac{3}{4} = 12\frac{1}{4}$

4. $3 \times 5\frac{1}{5} = 15\frac{3}{5}$ 5. $6 \times 3\frac{1}{6} = 19$ 6. $7 \times 2\frac{3}{5} = 18\frac{1}{5}$

7. $9 \times 3\frac{2}{3} = 33$ 8. $5 \times 6\frac{5}{8} = 33\frac{1}{8}$ 9. $4 \times 2\frac{1}{2} = 10$

10. $8 \times 9\frac{1}{10} = 72\frac{4}{5}$ 11. $3 \times 9\frac{1}{3} = 28$ 12. $7 \times 2\frac{1}{7} = 15$

Total Problems _12_ Problems Correct ____

© Carson-Dellosa CD-3747
68

Answer Key

Name_____   Skill: Multiplying Mixed Numbers
                                          and Whole Numbers

Multiply and write the answers in simplest form.

1. $4 \times 3\frac{3}{5} = 14\frac{2}{5}$ 2. $10 \times 5\frac{1}{2} = 55$ 3. $2 \times 5\frac{1}{8} = 10\frac{1}{4}$

4. $6 \times 9\frac{4}{5} = 58\frac{4}{5}$ 5. $8 \times 2\frac{3}{8} = 19$ 6. $3 \times 1\frac{15}{16} = 5\frac{13}{16}$

7. $2 \times 8\frac{3}{4} = 17\frac{1}{2}$ 8. $5 \times 4\frac{2}{5} = 22$ 9. $4 \times 8\frac{6}{7} = 35\frac{3}{7}$

10. $9 \times 1\frac{1}{18} = 9\frac{1}{2}$ 11. $2 \times 7\frac{5}{8} = 15\frac{1}{4}$ 12. $2 \times 2\frac{1}{4} = 4\frac{1}{2}$

Total Problems __12__ Problems Correct ____

69

Name_____   Skill: Multiplying Mixed Numbers

Multiply and write the answers in simplest form.

1. $3\frac{1}{2} \times 2\frac{1}{2} =$ 2. $2\frac{2}{3} \times 4\frac{2}{5} =$ 3. $6\frac{7}{8} \times 3\frac{1}{3} =$

   $8\frac{3}{4}$ $11\frac{11}{15}$ $22\frac{11}{12}$

4. $8\frac{5}{6} \times 3\frac{6}{7} =$ 5. $5\frac{3}{4} \times 6\frac{1}{4} =$ 6. $7\frac{9}{10} \times 8\frac{7}{8} =$

   $34\frac{1}{14}$ $35\frac{15}{16}$ $70\frac{9}{80}$

7. $4\frac{2}{5} \times 6\frac{2}{3} =$ 8. $2\frac{8}{9} \times 7\frac{7}{8} =$ 9. $4\frac{1}{4} \times 3\frac{5}{6} =$

   $29\frac{1}{3}$ $22\frac{3}{4}$ $16\frac{7}{24}$

10. $4\frac{2}{9} \times 5\frac{10}{11} =$ 11. $7\frac{1}{4} \times 3\frac{3}{7} =$ 12. $8\frac{3}{5} \times 1\frac{1}{2} =$

   $24\frac{94}{99}$ $24\frac{6}{7}$ $12\frac{9}{10}$

Total Problems __12__ Problems Correct ____

70

Name_____   Skill: Multiplying Mixed Numbers

Multiply and write the answers in simplest form.

1. $8\frac{1}{4} \times 6\frac{2}{3} = 55$

2. $5\frac{1}{5} \times 4\frac{1}{3} = 22\frac{8}{15}$

3. $7\frac{2}{5} \times 9\frac{1}{8} = 67\frac{21}{40}$

4. $9\frac{9}{10} \times 4\frac{7}{8} = 48\frac{21}{80}$

5. $2\frac{5}{6} \times 12\frac{4}{5} = 36\frac{4}{15}$

6. $1\frac{10}{13} \times 2\frac{9}{13} = 4\frac{129}{169}$

7. $4\frac{2}{7} \times 6\frac{1}{10} = 26\frac{1}{7}$

8. $8\frac{3}{5} \times 4\frac{5}{6} = 41\frac{17}{30}$

Total Problems __8__ Problems Correct ____

71

Name_____   Skill: Adding Decimals

Add.

1. $\begin{aligned}14.2\\ +\,12.1\\ \hline 26.3\end{aligned}$	2. $\begin{aligned}12.3\\ +\,15.2\\ \hline 27.5\end{aligned}$	3. $\begin{aligned}18.2\\ +\,16.5\\ \hline 34.7\end{aligned}$	4. $\begin{aligned}22.2\\ +\,13.1\\ \hline 35.3\end{aligned}$	5. $\begin{aligned}47.5\\ +\,32.6\\ \hline 80.1\end{aligned}$	6. $\begin{aligned}54.8\\ +\,13.2\\ \hline 68.0\end{aligned}$
7. $\begin{aligned}18.7\\ +\,10.5\\ \hline 29.2\end{aligned}$	8. $\begin{aligned}16.6\\ +\,13.8\\ \hline 30.4\end{aligned}$	9. $\begin{aligned}15.2\\ +\,13.0\\ \hline 28.2\end{aligned}$	10. $\begin{aligned}12.0\\ +\,14.9\\ \hline 26.9\end{aligned}$	11. $\begin{aligned}49.4\\ +\,11.1\\ \hline 60.5\end{aligned}$	12. $\begin{aligned}34.2\\ +\,17.2\\ \hline 51.4\end{aligned}$
13. $\begin{aligned}1.47\\ +\,6.54\\ \hline 8.01\end{aligned}$	14. $\begin{aligned}7.85\\ +\,9.41\\ \hline 17.26\end{aligned}$	15. $\begin{aligned}2.22\\ +\,3.94\\ \hline 6.16\end{aligned}$	16. $\begin{aligned}7.54\\ +\,2.24\\ \hline 9.78\end{aligned}$	17. $\begin{aligned}8.85\\ +\,7.33\\ \hline 16.18\end{aligned}$	

18. $12.95 + 5.06 =$ __20.7__   19. $16.3 + 35.7 =$ __6.5__

20. $13.8 + 6.9 =$ __121.69__   21. $3.25 + 3.25 =$ __103.54__

22. $46.02 + 75.67 =$ __90.35__   23. $87.01 + 16.53 =$ __43.03__

Total Problems __23__ Problems Correct ____

72

Answer Key

Name_____   Skill: Adding Decimals

Add.

1. 4.15
    6.20
    + 8.63
    18.98

2. 2.26
    3.43
    + 8.15
    13.84

3. 32.15
    64.23
    + 32.57
    128.95

4. 3.564
    1.508
    + 1.521
    6.593

5. 8.461
    .003
    + .212
    8.676

6. .491
    .320
    + .617
    1.428

7. 14.501
    62.037
    + 8.693
    85.231

8. 62.715
    1.307
    + .032
    64.054

9. 7.35
    33.421
    + 42.6
    83.371

10. 1.908
    .076
    + 22.444
    24.428

11. .179
    2.602
    + 62.561
    65.342

12. 7.35
    16.201
    + 2.9
    26.451

13. 8.16 + 15.204 + 35.8 = __59.164__

14. .007 + 1.12 + 5.978 = __7.105__

Total Problems _14_ Problems Correct ____

© Carson-Dellosa CD-3747

73

Name_____   Skill: Subtracting Decimals

Subtract.

1. 5.6
    − 3.2
    2.4

2. 7.8
    − 4.5
    3.3

3. 6.3
    − 4.1
    2.2

4. 8.6
    − 5.2
    3.4

5. 7.6
    − 3.2
    4.4

6. 10.4
    − 8.2
    2.2

7. 9.3
    − 7.5
    1.8

8. 8.7
    − 5.2
    3.5

9. 16.4
    − 8.2
    8.2

10. 26.7
    − 2.5
    24.2

11. 8.5
    − 3.5
    5.0

12. 86.5
    − 2.3
    84.2

13. 9.65
    − 4.22
    5.43

14. 75.4
    − 3.1
    72.3

15. 16.2
    − 4.1
    12.1

16. 72.5 − 63.7 = __8.8__

17. 8.1 − 6.5 = __1.6__

Total Problems _17_ Problems Correct ____

© Carson-Dellosa CD-3747

74

Name_____   Skill: Subtracting Decimals

Subtract.

1. 326.7
    − 42.8
    283.9

2. 1.589
    − .756
    .833

3. 52.07
    − 3.9
    48.17

4. 8.123
    − 6.017
    2.106

5. 1.978
    − 1.682
    .296

6. 14.021
    − 5.6
    8.421

7. 16.882
    − 9.3
    7.582

8. 7.57
    − 6.85
    .72

9. 18.9
    − 16.425
    2.475

10. 14.9
    − 3.2
    11.7

11. 19.5 − .001 = __19.499__

12. 28.4 − 4.62 = __23.78__

13. .501 − .332 = __.169__

14. 33.45 − 15.4 = __18.05__

15. 42.642 − 10.35 = __32.292__

16. 18.5 − 9.5 = __9__

Total Problems _16_ Problems Correct ____

© Carson-Dellosa CD-3747

75

Name_____   Skill: Multiplying Decimals

Multiply.

1. 5.2
    x 1.8
    9.36

2. 2.2
    x 4.4
    9.68

3. 1.3
    x 1.0
    1.3

4. 6.4
    x 2.5
    16

5. 5.4
    x 1.3
    7.02

6. 10.5
    x 6.6
    69.3

7. .12
    x 3.7
    .444

8. 7.1
    x .25
    1.775

9. 16.2
    x 1.1
    17.82

10. 6.6
    x 1.5
    9.9

11. 2.8
    x 9.9
    27.72

12. 5.20
    x .21
    1.092

13. 7.54
    x 2.77
    20.8858

14. 2.0
    x 2.1
    4.2

15. 4.44
    x .01
    .0444

16. .34 x .12 = __.0408__

17. 6.1 x 2.5 = __15.25__

18. 45.5 x 4.6 = __209.3__

19. 5.6 x 7.3 = __40.88__

Total Problems _19_ Problems Correct ____

© Carson-Dellosa CD-3747

76

Answer Key

Name_____ Skill: Dividing Decimals

Divide.

1. $2\overline{)8.44}$ = 4.22
2. $7\overline{)3.92}$ = .56
3. $6\overline{)3.6}$ = .6
4. $4\overline{)9.6}$ = 2.4

5. $5\overline{)1.25}$ = .25
6. $2\overline{)9.4}$ = 4.7
7. $7\overline{)3.92}$ = .56
8. $5\overline{).865}$ = .173

9. $14\overline{)1.218}$ = .087
10. $24\overline{)17.28}$ = .72
11. $46\overline{).2346}$ = .0051
12. $67\overline{)274.7}$ = 4.1

13. 38.6 ÷ 2 = __19.3__
14. 42.3 ÷ 3 = __14.1__

15. .6566 ÷ 67 = __.0098__
16. .7255 ÷ 5 = __.1451__

17. 166.4 ÷ 52 = __3.2__
18. 166.0 ÷ 10 = __16.6__

Total Problems __18__ Problems Correct ____

© Carson-Dellosa CD-3747   77

Name_____ Skill: Dividing Decimals

Divide.

1. $.8\overline{)64}$ = 80
2. $.5\overline{)35}$ = 70
3. $.3\overline{)9}$ = 30
4. $.12\overline{)360}$ = 3,000

5. $.25\overline{)100}$ = 400
6. $1.2\overline{)48}$ = 40
7. $9.6\overline{)82.8}$ = 8.625
8. $.23\overline{)2.185}$ = 9.5

9. $6.1\overline{)7.93}$ = 1.3
10. $5.3\overline{)42.4}$ = 8
11. $.17\overline{)3.23}$ = 19
12. $7.2\overline{)40.32}$ = 5.6

13. 64 ÷ .4 = __160__
14. 152 ÷ .8 = __190__

15. 4.9 ÷ .7 = __7__
16. .63 ÷ .3 = __2.1__

17. 15.2 ÷ .19 = __80__
18. 1.365 ÷ 2.1 = __.65__

Total Problems __18__ Problems Correct ____

© Carson-Dellosa CD-3747   78

Name_____ Skill: Changing Decimals to Fractions

Change each decimal to a fraction. Write your answer in simplest form.

1. .5 = $\frac{1}{2}$
2. .1 = $\frac{1}{10}$
3. .4 = $\frac{2}{5}$

4. .6 = $\frac{3}{5}$
5. .2 = $\frac{1}{5}$
6. .8 = $\frac{4}{5}$

7. .7 = $\frac{7}{10}$
8. 4.1 = $4\frac{1}{10}$
9. 5.2 = $5\frac{1}{5}$

10. 9.5 = $9\frac{1}{2}$
11. 3.6 = $3\frac{3}{5}$
12. 2.5 = $2\frac{1}{2}$

13. 1.8 = $1\frac{4}{5}$
14. 7.3 = $7\frac{3}{10}$
15. 6.5 = $6\frac{1}{2}$

16. 2.2 = $2\frac{1}{5}$
17. 3.9 = $3\frac{9}{10}$
18. 4.2 = $4\frac{1}{5}$

19. 6.2 = $6\frac{1}{5}$
20. 8.8 = $8\frac{4}{5}$
21. 4.1 = $4\frac{1}{10}$

22. 1.25 = $1\frac{1}{4}$
23. 2.50 = $2\frac{1}{2}$
24. 9.3 = $9\frac{3}{10}$

Total Problems __24__ Problems Correct ____

© Carson-Dellosa CD-3747   79

Name_____ Skill: Changing Decimals to Fractions

Change each decimal to a fraction. Write your answer in simplest form.

1. 8.2 = $8\frac{1}{5}$
2. 9.1 = $9\frac{1}{10}$
3. 7.6 = $7\frac{3}{5}$

4. 5.4 = $5\frac{2}{5}$
5. 10.6 = $10\frac{3}{5}$
6. 25.3 = $25\frac{3}{10}$

7. 48.2 = $48\frac{1}{5}$
8. .25 = $\frac{1}{4}$
9. .75 = $\frac{3}{4}$

10. .15 = $\frac{3}{20}$
11. .68 = $\frac{17}{25}$
12. 4.36 = $4\frac{9}{25}$

13. 25.32 = $25\frac{8}{25}$
14. 86.12 = $86\frac{3}{25}$
15. 9.45 = $9\frac{9}{20}$

16. 3.25 = $3\frac{1}{4}$
17. 6.5 = $6\frac{1}{2}$
18. 75.2 = $75\frac{1}{5}$

19. 30.2 = $30\frac{1}{5}$
20. 9.12 = $9\frac{3}{25}$
21. 25.2 = $25\frac{1}{5}$

22. .625 = $\frac{5}{8}$
23. .125 = $\frac{1}{8}$
24. 25.0 = 25

Total Problems __24__ Problems Correct ____

© Carson-Dellosa CD-3747   80

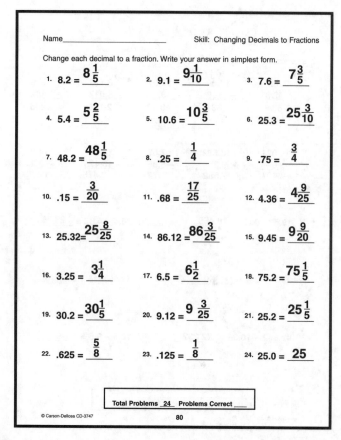

Answer Key

Name_____ Skill: Changing Fractions to Decimals

Change the fractions to decimals. Round to the nearest thousandth when necessary.

1. $\frac{5}{8}$ = **.625**   2. $\frac{1}{4}$ = **.25**   3. $\frac{3}{4}$ = **.75**

4. $\frac{1}{8}$ = **.125**   5. $\frac{7}{8}$ = **.875**   6. $\frac{5}{6}$ = **.833**

7. $\frac{1}{5}$ = **.2**   8. $\frac{4}{5}$ = **.8**   9. $\frac{9}{10}$ = **.9**

10. $\frac{1}{12}$ = **.083**   11. $\frac{2}{7}$ = **.286**   12. $\frac{11}{20}$ = **.55**

13. $\frac{1}{20}$ = **.05**   14. $\frac{3}{5}$ = **.6**   15. $\frac{1}{6}$ = **.167**

16. $\frac{5}{9}$ = **.556**   17. $\frac{3}{6}$ = **.5**   18. $\frac{8}{8}$ = **1**

Total Problems **18** Problems Correct ____

© Carson-Dellosa CD-3747
81

Name_____ Skill: Changing Fractions to Decimals and Decimals to Fractions

Complete the chart. Round to the nearest thousandth when necessary.

	Fraction	Decimal
1.	$\frac{1}{4}$	.25
2.	$\frac{1}{8}$	.125
3.	$\frac{1}{3}$	.334
4.	$\frac{5}{6}$	.834
5.	$\frac{7}{8}$	.875
6.	$\frac{111}{500}$	.222
7.	$\frac{9}{10}$	.9
8.	$\frac{1}{5}$	.2
9.	$\frac{3}{8}$	.375
10.	$\frac{4}{5}$	.8

Total Problems **10** Problems Correct ____

© Carson-Dellosa CD-3747
82

Name_____ Skill: Learning Lines and Line Segments

Circle the correct name for each of the following.

1. K——L   (Line KL)   Line Segment KL   Line K
2. F——D   Line FD   (Line Segment DF)   Line DF
3. A——B   Line BB   (Line Segment AB)   Line AB
4. C——F   Line CF   (Line Segment CF)   Line FC
5. E——M   Line MM   Line Segment EM   (Line EM)
6. N——P   Line NP   (Line Segment NP)   Line PN
7. O——R   (Line OR)   Line Segment OR   Line RO
8. S U   (Line SU)   Line Segment SU   Line S
9. V——X   Line V   (Line Segment VX)   Line VX
10. T——Q   (Line TQ)   Line Segment TQ   Line Q

Draw and label the following.

11. Line Segment BR   ●——————●
                        B   R
12. Line Segment ST   ●——————●
                        S   T
13. Line AB   ←———●——●———→
                    A   B

Total Problems **13** Problems Correct ____

© Carson-Dellosa CD-3747
83

Name_____ Skill: Naming Angles

Circle the correct names for the following angles.

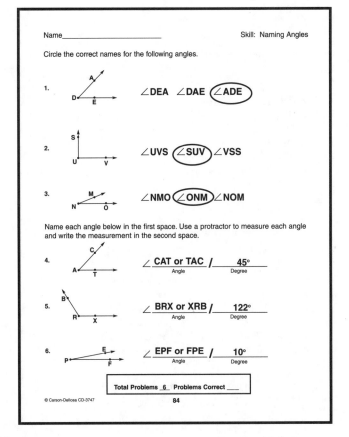

1. ∠DEA ∠DAE (∠ADE)

2. ∠UVS (∠SUV) ∠VSS

3. ∠NMO (∠ONM) ∠NOM

Name each angle below in the first space. Use a protractor to measure each angle and write the measurement in the second space.

4. ∠ **CAT or TAC** / **45°**
   Angle   Degree

5. ∠ **BRX or XRB** / **122°**
   Angle   Degree

6. ∠ **EPF or FPE** / **10°**
   Angle   Degree

Total Problems **6** Problems Correct ____

© Carson-Dellosa CD-3747
84

Answer Key

Name_____ Skill: Naming Polygons

Write the number of sides of each shape.

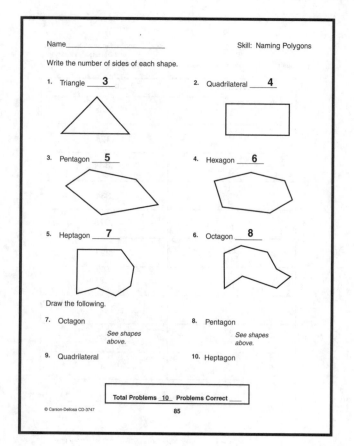

1. Triangle __3__
2. Quadrilateral __4__
3. Pentagon __5__
4. Hexagon __6__
5. Heptagon __7__
6. Octagon __8__

Draw the following.

7. Octagon   *See shapes above.*
8. Pentagon   *See shapes above.*
9. Quadrilateral
10. Heptagon

Total Problems __10__ Problems Correct ____

© Carson-Dellosa CD-3747
85

Name_____ Skill: Naming Circles and Polygons

Circle the correct name for the following figures.

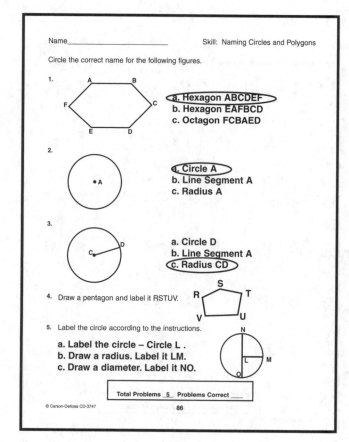

1.
    a. Hexagon ABCDEF (circled)
    b. Hexagon EAFBCD
    c. Octagon FCBAED

2.
    a. Circle A (circled)
    b. Line Segment A
    c. Radius A

3.
    a. Circle D
    b. Line Segment A
    c. Radius CD (circled)

4. Draw a pentagon and label it RSTUV.

5. Label the circle according to the instructions.
    a. Label the circle – Circle L .
    b. Draw a radius. Label it LM.
    c. Draw a diameter. Label it NO.

Total Problems __5__ Problems Correct ____

© Carson-Dellosa CD-3747
86

Name_____ Skill: Units of Measurement

Write the correct abbreviation in the blank.

1. **cm** centimeter   a. m
2. **yds** yard   b. cm
3. **ft** foot   c. mm
4. **km** kilometer   d. in
5. **in** inch   e. yd
6. **m** meter   f. mi
7. **mi** mile   g. ft
8. **mm** millimeter   h. km

Give the equivalents for the following.

9. 1 yd = __36__ in
10. 1 m = __100__ cm
11. 1 mi = __5,280__ ft
12. 1 cm = __.01__ m
13. 1 yd = __3__ ft
14. 1 km = __1,000__ m
15. 1 mi = __1,760__ yd
16. 1,000 m = __1__ km
17. 6 ft = __72__ in
18. 5 km = __5,000__ m
19. 3 mi = __5,280__ ya
20. 9 cm = __90__ mm
21. 2 yd = __72__ in
22. 300 mm = __30__ cm
23. 72 in = __6__ ft
24. 1 m = __.001__ km

Total Problems __24__ Problems Correct ____

© Carson-Dellosa CD-3747
87

Name_____ Skill: Finding Perimeters

Find the perimeter of each shape.

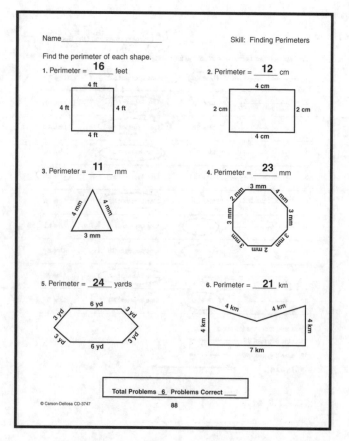

1. Perimeter = __16__ feet
2. Perimeter = __12__ cm
3. Perimeter = __11__ mm
4. Perimeter = __23__ mm
5. Perimeter = __24__ yards
6. Perimeter = __21__ km

Total Problems __6__ Problems Correct ____

© Carson-Dellosa CD-3747
88

Answer Key

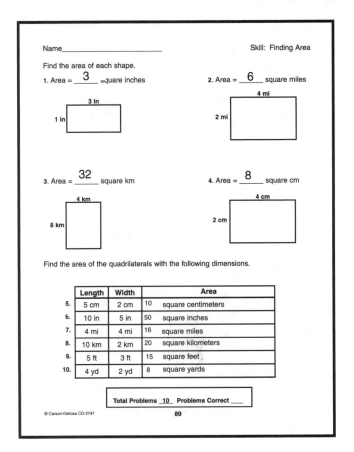

Name_____ Skill: Finding Area

Find the area of each shape.

1. Area = __3__ square inches

3 in
1 in

2. Area = __6__ square miles

4 mi
2 mi

3. Area = __32__ square km

4 km
8 km

4. Area = __8__ square cm

4 cm
2 cm

Find the area of the quadrilaterals with the following dimensions.

	Length	Width		Area
5.	5 cm	2 cm	10	square centimeters
6.	10 in	5 in	50	square inches
7.	4 mi	4 mi	16	square miles
8.	10 km	2 km	20	square kilometers
9.	5 ft	3 ft	15	square feet
10.	4 yd	2 yd	8	square yards

Total Problems _10_ Problems Correct ____

© Carson-Dellosa CD-3747
89

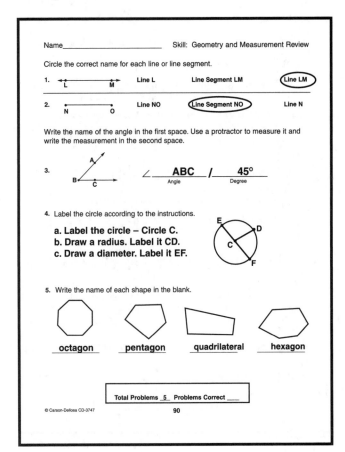

Name_____ Skill: Geometry and Measurement Review

Circle the correct name for each line or line segment.

1. L————M   Line L   Line Segment LM   (Line LM)

2. N————O   Line NO   (Line Segment NO)   Line N

Write the name of the angle in the first space. Use a protractor to measure it and write the measurement in the second space.

3. ∠ __ABC__ / __45°__
Angle   Degree

4. Label the circle according to the instructions.

a. Label the circle – Circle C.
b. Draw a radius. Label it CD.
c. Draw a diameter. Label it EF.

5. Write the name of each shape in the blank.

__octagon__   __pentagon__   __quadrilateral__   __hexagon__

Total Problems _5_ Problems Correct ____

© Carson-Dellosa CD-3747
90

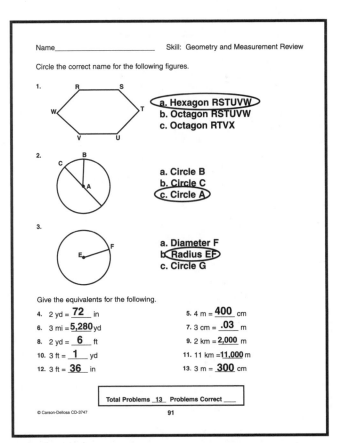

Name_____ Skill: Geometry and Measurement Review

Circle the correct name for the following figures.

1.
R—S
W   T
V—U
a. Hexagon RSTUVW
b. Octagon RSTUVW
c. Octagon RTVX

2.
a. Circle B
b. Circle C
c. Circle A

3.
a. Diameter F
b. Radius EF
c. Circle G

Give the equivalents for the following.

4. 2 yd = __72__ in
5. 4 m = __400__ cm
6. 3 mi = __5,280__ yd
7. 3 cm = __.03__ m
8. 2 yd = __6__ ft
9. 2 km = __2,000__ m
10. 3 ft = __1__ yd
11. 11 km = __11,000__ m
12. 3 ft = __36__ in
13. 3 m = __300__ cm

Total Problems _13_ Problems Correct ____

© Carson-Dellosa CD-3747
91

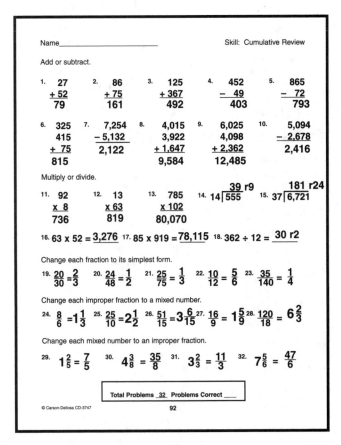

Name_____ Skill: Cumulative Review

Add or subtract.

1. $\begin{array}{r} 27 \\ + 52 \\ \hline 79 \end{array}$
2. $\begin{array}{r} 86 \\ + 75 \\ \hline 161 \end{array}$
3. $\begin{array}{r} 125 \\ + 367 \\ \hline 492 \end{array}$
4. $\begin{array}{r} 452 \\ - 49 \\ \hline 403 \end{array}$
5. $\begin{array}{r} 865 \\ - 72 \\ \hline 793 \end{array}$

6. $\begin{array}{r} 325 \\ 415 \\ + 75 \\ \hline 815 \end{array}$
7. $\begin{array}{r} 7,254 \\ - 5,132 \\ \hline 2,122 \end{array}$
8. $\begin{array}{r} 4,015 \\ 3,922 \\ + 1,647 \\ \hline 9,584 \end{array}$
9. $\begin{array}{r} 6,025 \\ 4,098 \\ + 2,362 \\ \hline 12,485 \end{array}$
10. $\begin{array}{r} 5,094 \\ - 2,678 \\ \hline 2,416 \end{array}$

Multiply or divide.

11. $\begin{array}{r} 92 \\ \times 8 \\ \hline 736 \end{array}$
12. $\begin{array}{r} 13 \\ \times 63 \\ \hline 819 \end{array}$
13. $\begin{array}{r} 785 \\ \times 102 \\ \hline 80,070 \end{array}$
14. $14\overline{\smash)555}$ 39 r9
15. $37\overline{\smash)6,721}$ 181 r24

16. 63 x 52 = __3,276__
17. 85 x 919 = __78,115__
18. 362 ÷ 12 = __30 r2__

Change each fraction to its simplest form.

19. $\frac{20}{30} = \frac{2}{3}$
20. $\frac{24}{48} = \frac{1}{2}$
21. $\frac{25}{75} = \frac{1}{3}$
22. $\frac{10}{12} = \frac{5}{6}$
23. $\frac{35}{140} = \frac{1}{4}$

Change each improper fraction to a mixed number.

24. $\frac{8}{6} = 1\frac{1}{3}$
25. $\frac{25}{10} = 2\frac{1}{2}$
26. $\frac{51}{15} = 3\frac{6}{15}$
27. $\frac{16}{9} = 1\frac{5}{9}$
28. $\frac{120}{18} = 6\frac{2}{3}$

Change each mixed number to an improper fraction.

29. $1\frac{2}{5} = \frac{7}{5}$
30. $4\frac{3}{8} = \frac{35}{8}$
31. $3\frac{2}{3} = \frac{11}{3}$
32. $7\frac{5}{6} = \frac{47}{6}$

Total Problems _32_ Problems Correct ____

© Carson-Dellosa CD-3747
92

© Carson-Dellosa CD-3747

118

Answer Key

Make each pair of fractions equivalent.

1. $\frac{1}{3} = \frac{6}{18}$ 2. $\frac{6}{7} = \frac{36}{42}$ 3. $\frac{9}{10} = \frac{45}{50}$ 4. $\frac{3}{4} = \frac{15}{20}$ 5. $\frac{3}{5} = \frac{15}{25}$

Add or subtract the fractions and mixed numbers. Change to simplest form.

6. $\frac{3}{7} + \frac{2}{7} = \frac{5}{7}$ 7. $\frac{1}{5} + \frac{4}{5} = 1$ 8. $\frac{6}{6} + \frac{3}{3} = 2$ 9. $\frac{15}{17} + \frac{16}{17} = 1\frac{14}{17}$

10. $4\frac{1}{4} - 2\frac{3}{4} = 1\frac{1}{2}$ 11. $3\frac{3}{9} + 4\frac{5}{18} = 7\frac{11}{18}$ 12. $2\frac{2}{5} + 3\frac{3}{15} = 5\frac{9}{15}$

Multiply the fractions and mixed numbers. Change to simplest form.

13. $\frac{5}{7} \times \frac{2}{7} = \frac{10}{49}$ 14. $2 \times \frac{1}{3} = \frac{2}{3}$ 15. $\frac{5}{8} \times \frac{3}{8} = \frac{15}{64}$ 16. $\frac{1}{2} \times \frac{4}{5} = \frac{2}{5}$

17. $4\frac{1}{4} \times 2\frac{3}{4} = 11\frac{11}{16}$ 18. $2\frac{7}{8} \times 6\frac{2}{3} = 19\frac{1}{6}$ 19. $2\frac{3}{5} \times 5\frac{1}{2} = 14\frac{3}{10}$

Add or subtract.

20. $3.1 + 6.2 = 9.3$ 21. $5.9 + 4.2 = 10.1$ 22. $74.06 - 3.1 = 70.96$ 23. $86.29 + .03 = 86.32$ 24. $406.34 - 26.12 = 380.22$

25. $42.5 + 1.8 = 44.3$ 26. $34.23 + 16.5 = 50.73$

27. $13.1 + 5.5 = 18.6$ 28. $45.31 - 17.2 = 28.11$

Total Problems __28__ Problems Correct ____

© Carson-Dellosa CD-3747 93

Multiply or divide.

1. $12 \times 3.4 = 40.8$ 2. $23 \times .16 = 3.68$ 3. $9.63 \times 12.2 = 117.486$ 4. $.953 \times .7 = .6671$ 5. $.75 \times .3 = .225$

6. $5\overline{)18.5} = 3.7$ 7. $.27\overline{)224.1} = 830$ 8. $8\overline{)25.6} = 3.2$ 9. $16\overline{)89.6} = 5.6$

10. $12 \times 1.2 = \underline{14.4}$ 11. $2.84 \times 16.5 = \underline{46.86}$

12. $89.6 \div 16 = \underline{5.6}$ 13. $25.6 \div 8 = \underline{3.2}$

14. $.75 \times 3 = \underline{2.25}$ 15. $.3 \times 75 = \underline{22.5}$

16. $.996 \div 12 = \underline{.083}$ 17. $30 \div .25 = \underline{120}$

18. $.721 \div 7 = \underline{.103}$ 19. $10 \div .20 = \underline{50}$

20. $.50 \div 2 = \underline{.25}$ 21. $70 \div .35 = \underline{200}$

Total Problems __21__ Problems Correct ____

© Carson-Dellosa CD-3747 94

Change each decimal to a fraction.

1. $5.2 = 5\frac{1}{5}$ 2. $.5 = \frac{1}{2}$ 3. $6.4 = 6\frac{2}{5}$ 4. $2.52 = 2\frac{13}{25}$ $12.36 = 12\frac{9}{25}$

Change each fraction or mixed number to a decimal.

6. $\frac{1}{8} = .125$ 7. $\frac{3}{4} = .75$ 8. $2\frac{3}{8} = 2.375$ 9. $5\frac{3}{4} = 5.75$ 10. $3\frac{3}{5} = 3.6$

Draw and label the following.

11. Line Segment ST

12. Line PQ

13. Angle XYZ

14. Pentagon EFGHI

15. Circle G, with Radius GH

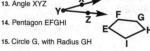

Fill in the blank with the correct equivalent.

16. 1 yard = __3__ feet

17. 1 foot = __12__ inches

18. 1 mile = __1,760__ yards

19. 1 yard = __36__ inches

20. 1 meter = __100__ centimeters

21. 1 centimeter = __.01__ meters

22. 1 meter = __1,000__ kilometers

Total Problems __22__ Problems Correct ____

© Carson-Dellosa CD-3747 95

Add.

$$4{,}888 \atop + \underline{247}$$

Subtract.

$$62 \atop - \underline{9}$$

Multiply.

$$2 \atop \underline{\times \ 9}$$

Multiply.

$$515 \atop \underline{\times \ \ 4}$$

Add.

$$9{,}841 \atop + \underline{520}$$

Add.

$$7{,}732 \atop 806 \atop 54 \atop + \underline{325}$$

Multiply.

$$8 \atop \underline{\times \ 8}$$

Multiply.

$$28 \atop \underline{\times \ 3}$$

Add.

$$53 \atop + \underline{\ 53}$$

Add.

$$143 \atop 225 \atop + \underline{\ 336}$$

Subtract.

$$72{,}541 \atop - \underline{8{,}530}$$

Multiply.

$$21 \atop \underline{\times \ 3}$$

Add.

$$25 \atop + \underline{\ 5}$$

Add.

$$3{,}804 \atop + \underline{207}$$

Subtract.

$$800 \atop - \underline{\ 72}$$

Multiply.

$$7 \atop \underline{\times \ 10}$$

5,135	53	18	2,060
10,361	8,917	64	84
106	704	64,011	63
30	4,011	728	70

Multiply.

542
x 172

© CD-3747

Multiply.

216
x 10

© CD-3747

Multiply.

53
x 38

© CD-3747

Multiply.

3,232
x 4

© CD-3747

Divide.

$2\overline{)39}$

© CD-3747

Divide.

$5\overline{)90}$

© CD-3747

Divide.

$4\overline{)54}$

© CD-3747

Divide.

$3\overline{)12}$

© CD-3747

Divide.

$37\overline{)369}$

© CD-3747

Divide.

$52\overline{)624}$

© CD-3747

Divide.

$5\overline{)943}$

© CD-3747

Divide.

$4\overline{)1,228}$

© CD-3747

Fill in the circle with <, >, or =.

$\frac{16}{20} \bigcirc \frac{10}{25}$

© CD-3747

Change to simplest form.

$\frac{7}{14} =$

© CD-3747

Change to simplest form.

$\frac{3}{24} =$

© CD-3747

Divide.

$48\overline{)2,541}$

© CD-3747

93,224

19 r1

9 r36

>

2,160

18

12

$\frac{1}{2}$

2,014

13 r2

188 r3

$\frac{1}{8}$

12,928

4

307

52 r45

Change to a mixed number.

$$\frac{40}{24} =$$

Change to a mixed number.

$$\frac{19}{5} =$$

Change to a mixed number.

$$\frac{21}{12} =$$

Change to a mixed number.

$$\frac{20}{15} =$$

Find the equivalent.

$$6 = \frac{}{5}$$

Find the equivalent.

$$\frac{8}{9} = \frac{}{54}$$

Change to an improper fraction.

$$10\frac{5}{6} =$$

Change to an improper fraction.

$$7\frac{4}{5} =$$

Multiply.

$$8 \times \frac{1}{7} =$$

Multiply.

$$2 \times \frac{2}{5} =$$

Multiply.

$$\frac{3}{5} \times \frac{2}{9} =$$

Multiply.

$$\frac{7}{8} \times \frac{1}{6} =$$

Multiply.

$$8\frac{5}{6} \times 3\frac{6}{7} =$$

Multiply.

$$6 \times 9\frac{4}{5} =$$

Multiply.

$$3 \times 5\frac{1}{5} =$$

Multiply.

$$4 \times \frac{4}{7} =$$

$34\frac{1}{14}$	$1\frac{1}{7}$	30	$1\frac{2}{3}$
$58\frac{4}{5}$	$\frac{4}{5}$	48	$3\frac{4}{5}$
$15\frac{3}{5}$	$\frac{2}{15}$	$\frac{65}{6}$	$1\frac{3}{4}$
$2\frac{2}{7}$	$\frac{7}{48}$	$\frac{39}{5}$	$1\frac{1}{3}$

Multiply.

$$7\frac{2}{5} \times 9\frac{1}{8} =$$

Add.

$$\frac{2}{9} + \frac{5}{9} =$$

Add.

$$\begin{array}{r}\frac{6}{8}\\[-2pt]+\ \frac{1}{8}\\\hline\end{array}$$

Add.

$$5\frac{2}{7} + 6\frac{4}{7} =$$

Add.

$$\begin{array}{r}2\frac{2}{5}\\[-2pt]+\ 6\frac{4}{5}\\\hline\end{array}$$

Add.

$$\begin{array}{r}\frac{1}{3}\\[-2pt]+\ \frac{5}{6}\\\hline\end{array}$$

Add.

$$\begin{array}{r}\frac{2}{3}\\[-2pt]+\ \frac{3}{4}\\\hline\end{array}$$

Add.

$$\begin{array}{r}2\frac{5}{6}\\[-2pt]+\ 6\frac{3}{4}\\\hline\end{array}$$

Add.

$$\begin{array}{r}3\frac{11}{12}\\[-2pt]+\ 4\frac{1}{2}\\\hline\end{array}$$

Add.

$$2\frac{3}{4} + 7\frac{1}{3} =$$

Add.

$$\begin{array}{r}\frac{4}{5}\\[-2pt]+\ \frac{7}{8}\\\hline\end{array}$$

Subtract.

$$\begin{array}{r}\frac{7}{12}\\[-2pt]-\ \frac{5}{12}\\\hline\end{array}$$

Subtract.

$$\frac{5}{9} - \frac{2}{9} =$$

Subtract.

$$\begin{array}{r}4\\[-2pt]-\ \frac{3}{10}\\\hline\end{array}$$

Subtract.

$$\begin{array}{r}9\\[-2pt]-\ 3\frac{3}{11}\\\hline\end{array}$$

Subtract.

$$\begin{array}{r}4\frac{2}{6}\\[-2pt]-\ 3\frac{5}{6}\\\hline\end{array}$$

$11\frac{6}{7}$

$9\frac{7}{12}$

$\frac{1}{6}$

$\frac{1}{2}$

$\frac{7}{8}$

$1\frac{5}{12}$

$1\frac{27}{40}$

$8\frac{8}{11}$

$\frac{7}{9}$

$1\frac{1}{6}$

$10\frac{1}{12}$

$3\frac{7}{10}$

$67\frac{21}{40}$

$9\frac{1}{5}$

$8\frac{5}{12}$

$\frac{1}{3}$

Subtract.

$$4\frac{1}{3} - 2\frac{3}{8}$$

Subtract.

$$10.4 - 8.2$$

Subtract.

$$16.882 - 9.3$$

Multiply.

$$.12 \times 3.7$$

Subtract.

$$\frac{13}{15} - \frac{2}{3}$$

Add.

$$8.461 + .003 + .212$$

Subtract.

$$86.5 - 2.3$$

Multiply.

$$10.5 \times 6.6$$

Subtract.

$$\frac{3}{4} - \frac{1}{5}$$

Add.

$$18.7 + 10.5$$

Subtract.

$$8.5 - 3.5$$

Subtract.

$$14.021 - 5.6$$

Subtract.

$$2\frac{2}{3} - 2\frac{1}{3}$$

Subtract.

$$4\frac{7}{10} - 1\frac{4}{5}$$

Subtract.

$$9.3 - 7.5$$

Subtract.

$$7.57 - 6.85$$

$1\frac{23}{24}$

2.2

7.582

.444

$\frac{1}{5}$

8.676

84.2

69.3

$\frac{11}{20}$

29.2

5.0

8.421

$\frac{1}{3}$

$2\frac{9}{10}$

1.8

.72

Multiply.

$$\begin{array}{r} 7.1 \\ \times\ .25 \\ \hline \end{array}$$

Multiply.

$$\begin{array}{r} 16.2 \\ \times\ 1.1 \\ \hline \end{array}$$

Multiply.

$$\begin{array}{r} 6.6 \\ \times\ 1.5 \\ \hline \end{array}$$

Multiply.

$$\begin{array}{r} 3.3 \\ \times\ 2.2 \\ \hline \end{array}$$

Divide.

$14\overline{)1.218}$

Divide.

$24\overline{)17.28}$

Divide.

$46\overline{).2346}$

Change to a fraction.

.5

Change to a fraction.

.125

Change to a decimal.

$\dfrac{1}{8}$

Change to a decimal.

$\dfrac{1}{4}$

Find the area.

3 in
1 in

Find the perimeter.

4 ft
3 ft
4 ft
3 ft

Identify.

K   L

Identify.

D   R

Identify.

A
D
E

7.26

$\frac{1}{2}$

3in ^{2}

$\angle$ ADE
$\angle$ EDA

9.9

.0051

.25

Line DR

17.82

.72

.125

Line KL

1.775

.087

$\frac{1}{8}$

14 ft